Guyana's
TASTY EXOTIC

FOODS OF SIX PEOPLES

A CONTEMPORARY TAKE ON THE CUISINE OF
GUYANA, THE LAND OF SIX PEOPLES.

Copyright © 2010 by Deborah Barocas . 584557

Library of Congress Control Number: 2010903339

ISBN: Softcover 978-1-4500-5944-2
Hardcover 978-1-4500-5945-9
EBook 978-1-9845-6478-8

All rights reserved. No part of this book may be reproduced or transmitted in any form or by any means, electronic or mechanical, including photocopying, recording, or by any information storage and retrieval system, without permission in writing from the copyright owner.

Print information available on the last page

Rev. date: 11/05/2018

To order additional copies of this book, contact:
Xlibris
1-888-795-4274
www.Xlibris.com
Orders@Xlibris.com

Contents

Introduction	5
Aunt Savitri's Petha	6
Bakes	6
Banana Fritters	7
Bara	7
Beef Patties	8
Black Cake	9
Black Eye Peas Cook-Up Rice	10
Black Pudding	11
Blueberry Pie with a Pineapple Twist	12
Callaloo Cook-Up	13
Canton Char Sui/Cantonese Barbeque Pork Belly	14
Caribbean BBQ Sauce	14
Caribbean Pineapple Holiday Ham	15
Caribbean SheCrab Soup	16
Caribe Banana Muffins	16
Chan Jairam's Cassava Pone	17
Pineapple Rum Chicken ala Caribbean	17
Cheese Rolls	18
Cheese Straws	18
Chicken Biryani	19
Chicken Lo Mein	20
Chicken Soup (a.k.a. Jewish Penicillin)	21
Matzo Balls My Way	22
Chocolate Chip Scones	23
Coriander and Mint chutney	23
Cornish Pasties	24
Cottage Pie	25
Cow feet Souse	26
Creolese Grilled Shrimp	26
Curried Chicken With Potatoes	27
Caribbean Goat Curry	28
Dhal Puri	29
Dumplings	30
Eggnog	30
Fish Cakes	31
Fish Masala	32
Fish Pie with Cheese	32
Foo Foo	33
Fooncee	33
Savory Fried Okra Fritters	36
Fried Shark	36
Garam Masala for Meat	37
Garlic Pork/Lamb/Beef/Chicken	38
Ginger Beer	39
Guyanese Pepper Sauce	39
Portuguese Beef Stew	40
Guyanese Cantonese Fried Rice	41
Kedgeree	42
Killer Mojito Recipe	43
Lai Fun (Chinese Soup)	43

Mango Sour Condiment	44
Mauby Beverage	44
Mettemgee	45
Mom's Flaming Hot Pepper Sauce	46
Mom's Guyanese Bread	46
My fit for a Goddess Pot Roast	47
Pan Fried Okra with Shrimp	48
Orange Ginger Roast Pork Loin	49
Paratha Roti	49
Pastry Dough	50
Pepperpot	50
Phulourie	51
Ham, Cheese & Herb Scones	51
Pineapple Galette with Cherry Jelly Glaze	52
Sweet Pastry Dough	52
Martin's Favorite Potted Chicken	53
Pub style Beef and Stout Pie	54
Pulao	55
Pumpkin Pie	55
Roasted Red Snapper	56
Roath	57
Salara	57
Salt Cod with Potatoes and Eggs	58
Salt Fish Cakes	58
Shepherds Pie	59
Shrimp Exotic	59
Tuesday Shrove Pancakes	60
Siew Yuk (Cantonese Crispy Roast Pork)	61
Sizzling Ginger Chicken	62
Sorrel Beverage	62
Spicy Sweet Wing Dings	63
Split Pea Soup	63
Split Peas Cook-up	64
Split Peas Creole Soup	64
Savory Stuffed Cabbage	65
Stuffed Eggplants	66
Sweet Lobster Pomegranate Salad	67
Tropical Sangria with nectars du jour	67
Chan's Diwali Kheer (Sweet Rice)	68
Tamarind Chutney	68
Callaloo Cook-Up	69
Yeung Chow Fried Rice	70
Cantonese Style Orange Chicken	71
Caribe Shrimp Roll	71
Cucumber Tea Sandwiches	72
Spicy & Sweet Guava BBQ Sauce	72
Curried Fish	73
Fish Quiche	74
Peas and Rice Caribe Style	75
Caribbean Kitchen Reference	76
Glossary	78

Lush forests, magnificent waterfalls, fruits and foods of exotic flavors, celebrate the heritage of the land of many waters, also known as Guyana.

Colonized first by the Dutch, then the British, Guyana became independent of the United Kingdom in May of 1966. Situated on the northeast corner of the South American continent, this unique English- speaking country boasts the largest unspoilt rainforest in that region of the world. This tropical paradise is defined by its many natural wealthy resources namely sugar, rice, bauxite, and gold, just to list a few. Its rainforests are laden with unique medicinal herbs, rare animals, as an abundance of untapped resources stands preserved in its pristine environment.

Over the last decade or so, Guyana has become more diverse with immigrants from Brazil, Columbia, Jamaica, and many other countries. This can only make for a larger pot of exotic stew to sweep this nation into a culinary renaissance. Now residing in New York City, I enjoy the expansion of culinaris in my kitchen from its melting pot society, but can only imagine what the new immigrants are bringing to Guyana's already ethnically infused table to further enrich, flavor, and decorate their already exotic smorgasbord.

My beautiful Guyana known as the land of six peoples, consists of Indigenous people known as Amerindians, Africans, Indians, Portuguese, Chinese, and Europeans. Together we've shared a love of foods, music, and traditions taken from each ethnic background, and ultimately molded it into a magnetic sphere that represents us a whole. I invite you to join me in discovering and rediscovering some of the old classic recipes reflecting Guyanese foods, and explore some of the new ones creating in my kitchen.

Dedicated to my precious sons
Martin and Matthew

**To my Mom Vera and my late grandmother Violet
who were fantastic cooks, and influenced
my culinary expertise greatly**

In Guyana after immigrants arrived, they continued many of their traditions, but first generation Guyanese sometimes didn't quite pronounce or spell some things the same way their foreparents did from the old country. Often times, names of foods or ingredients were spelt or pronounced differently. For example what is known in India as Petha, is referred to as Perah in Guyana. My Uncle Nizam brought some the best Petha from a place called Cane Groove Village, and I was lucky to meet Tanuja Ragoo's Aunt Savitri who makes Petha the way I remembered it.

Aunt Savitri's Petha

1 tin of condensed milk
1 cup of white sugar
½ tbspn ground cardamom

Method:

Combine all ingredients in a saucepot

Bring to a boil on medium heat

Reduce and simmer on a low flame

Cook for about 15 minutes stirring constantly

Remove from stove and continue stirring

Start a whipping method using a wooden spoon

Whip to achieve a thickening texture

Continue whipping and remove heat

This will thicken and appear leave the sides of the sauce pot in folds

The mixture will take on a somewhat solidifying effect

Fill a small bowl of water, and set aside

Moisten hands

Using a teaspoon, dip and fill it

Transfer it into the palm of your hand

Mold into a patty or small nugget

Place these molds on a sheet pan lined with

greased proof or freezer paper to cool before serving

Bakes

Bakes are fried breads that are delicious by themselves, but can be eaten with an accompaniment. When my Mom made bakes, she paired it with many different sides. Sometimes it was salted fish(Bacahlau) stir fried with tomatoes, onions, garlic, hot pepper, or sometimes a piece of fried fish, or eggs. Enjoy them whichever way you choose, but try to eat them while they are still hot.

2 cups of all purpose flour
1 ½ tsp baking powder
1 tsp salt
2 tbsp brown sugar
2 tbsp of unsalted butter
1 ½ cups of water
2 cups of vegetable oil

Method:

Heat oil in a deep-frying pans on medium heat

Measure all ingredients, and sift together into a mixing bowl

Using fingers, rub butter into flour until combine well

Pour water a little at a time until all the mixture forms a soft dough

Cut into six equal parts and form into a round ball

Sprinkle flour on a dry surface

Using a rolling pin, roll into a five inch (diameter) disk

Transfer the Bake into the frying pan

Fry on side for one minute and flip

Fry on the other side for another minute or until brown

Transfer to a place covered with a soft cloth

Serve immediately by slitting Bake with a knife to create an opening

Stuff with your favorite fillings.

Banana Fritters

3 big yellow bananas
1 cup all purpose flour
6 tbsp sugar
½ tsp grated nutmeg
½ tsp ground cinnamon
1/8 tsp kosher salt
½ tsp baking soda
1 tsp vanilla essence
½ cup milk
1 egg
½ cup oil

Method:

In a bowl sift all dry ingredients

Whisk egg with vanilla

Add milk to mixture to form a thick batter

Slice bananas into 2" thick rounds

Heat oil to 400 degrees in a deep frying pan

Drop banana pieces 6 at a time into the batter and coat well

Gently add pieces using a wooden spoon to hot oil

Turn after 1 minute on each side or until golden brown

Remove and dust with powdered sugar

Bara

½ pt split peas (soaked overnight)
3 ½ cups all purpose flour
1/4 tsp black pepper
2 tbsp baking powder
2 tbsp salt
1 tsp dried yeast
1/4 tsp seasoning salt (optional)
1 ½ tsp garlic powder
2 tbsp freshly ground garlic
1 medium yellow onion (pureed)
1 scotch bonnet pepper or 3 wiri wiri peppers (pureed)
2 blades of chopped scallion
1 ½ tbsp turmeric
1 tbsp geera (cumin)
4 cups vegetable oil
1 cup warm water

Method:

In a blender add split peas and 1 cup of water and puree

Transfer into a mixing bowl

Add all other ingredients

Let this rest for 30 minutes

Add vegetable oil in frying pan and heat to 400 degrees

Scoop 1 tbsp of batter and form into a small disk shape

Lower hand and drop gently into hot oil

Cook for two minutes on each side

Remove and place on a double folded paper towel to absorb excess oil

Serve with mango sour condiment (found in index)

As a teenager, whenever I walked down Camp Street in Georgetown, I was always lured into the Nook Café by the intoxicating smells that drifted out and beckoned me in for a bite of a Beef Patty, Cheese Roll, or Pine Tart. The Nook's Beef Patty is in a class of its own, and I have not tasted anything similar. So in my quest to duplicate this recipe, I believe that I have come quite close, if not exact to its original flavor. You be the judge if you have had a Nook Beef Patty. Sadly, the Nook Cafe no longer exists, so work with me on this one…please.

Beef Patties

1 lb of ground chuck
1 (8 oz) can of sweet green peas
2 beef bouillon
1 tbsp Worcestershire sauce
1 yellow onion minced finely
2 tbsp fresh chopped thyme
4-6 wiri wiri peppers or ½ minced habernero
3 tbsp finely minced celery leaves
2 blades of scallion minced
1 tsp allspice
1 tsp ground coriander
½ tsp salt
1 tbsp vegetable oil
Pastry dough recipe doubled (see index for recipe)
Egg wash(consisting of 1 egg beaten and 1 tbsp water)

Method:
Season meat with salt, pepper, Worcestershire sauce, onion, allspice, wiri wiri pepper, and coriander

In a skillet, add oil and heat then add meat and bouillon

Saute on high heat or 2 minutes

Add thyme, sweet green peas, and continue to cook for 1 minute

Remove immediately in order to have a half cooked meat mixture

Bring to room temperature

Add scallions and celery leaves and incorporate using a spatula

Roll out pastry dough and cut rounds using a biscuit cutter

Fill center with approximately 1 ½ tbsp meat filling

Brush egg wash around the edges, top with another round of pastry dough

Press to seal edges with fingers, then use a fork to create indentations on edge

This will create a nice finish

Finally, prick the top with a fork, and baste with egg wash

Place on a greased flat sheet pan, and bake at 375 degrees for 25 minutes

Cool on a rack, but serve warm

It's Christmas morning, I can smell the Pepperpot simmering, the freshly baked Bread, the Garlic Pork frying, and the Black Cake aromas that still lingers from the night before. Everything in the house is pristine, chimes of carols spawn across the many homes, and the day that everyone has worked hard to prepare for has finally arrived. Have your breakfast, the Black Cake can wait.

Black Cake

Marinated Dried Fruits for Fruit Cake
1 ½ lbs pitted prunes
1 lb currants
½ lb cherries
750 ml bottle of dark rum
1 small bottle of Brandy
1 lbs raisins
½ lb citron
2 ozs of almond paste or ground almonds
1 medium sized bottle of port wine

Method:
Place fruits and almond paste or ground almonds into a large wide mouth glass jar

Add rum, port, and wine

Stir and cover

Let this sit and macerate for 1 month

Submerge a hand held blender into the jar and pulse to grind

Or use a grinding method that works for you, like a food processor of a food mill

Continue until the fruits are grounded and blended together

If fruits are not very moist after grinding, add 4 ozs of port wine, but must remain in a thick paste consistency. Store in a cool place for up to 2 years or more, check periodically to add port or rum

For the cake
4 cups of all purpose flour
1 lb butter(4 sticks) (at room temp.)
8 eggs
2 tsp ground cinnamon
1 tsp Angostura bitters
2 tbsp baking powder
1 tbsp vanilla essence
2 cups of dark brown sugar
1 tsp ground clove
3 tbsp black strap molasses

Heat oven to 350 degrees
In a large mixing bowl or a cake mixer, mix sugar and butter until creamy and light
Add eggs two at a time, until all the eggs are used up
Add vanilla, cinnamon, clove, molasses, and angostura bitters and continue to mix
Add flour and baking powder increments, and carefully fold in rum soaked fruits
Check texture of cake by positioning a spoon to stand self supported, if it falls, add more flour
Be careful to add small amounts of flour, and fold it, then retest the standing spoon process
Pour mixture into greased and floured 9" cake pans, and bake for 90 minutes. Insert a toothpick to check for doneness. If it comes out covered with wet batter, continue to bake until insertion comes out mostly clean. Some moistness is required to ensure a perfect end result
While this is hot, pour a cup of wine or whisky and let this rest for 1 week (purely optional)

Black Eye Peas Cook-Up Rice

2 cups of long grain rice
1 cup of black eye peas (soaked overnight)
½ lb of salted beef (optional)
1 lb of pickled pigtails (optional)
1 lb beef (with bones preferred)
3 cups of water
2 cups of coconut milk
1 tbsp of finely chopped thyme
1 medium onion minced finely
1 scotch bonnet pepper minced finely
1/4 tsp ground black pepper
1 tbsp casereep or soy (optional)
2 small or 1 large bouillon cubes
1 tsp ground allspice
½ tsp salt
2 tbsp of oil

Method:
In a soup pot, bring pigtails and salt beef to a rapid boil

Reduce heat and simmer for 40 minutes

Discard liquid and set aside

Heat 1 tbsp oil and add black eye peas

Cook until slightly brown

Add 1 tbsp of casereep or soy and allspice

Continue to cook until it's absorbed

Pour in 2 cups of water

Bring to a rapid boil and reduce to a simmer

Cook black eyes peas for 30 minutes or until cooked but firm

Transfer to a bowl and set aside

Add to 1 tbsp oil, chopped onion and saute

Add beef and saute until all liquid sprung from meat has been absorbed

Add pigtails and salted beef, and cook for 2 minutes

Add rice, scotch bonnet pepper, thyme, black pepper, bouillon,

salt, coconut milk, cooked black eye peas, and the additional water

Incorporate well by stirring and bring to a rapid boil

Reduce to a low fire and simmer for 20 minutes

Fluff with a fork and transfer to a serving platter

** If using canned coconut milk, add 2 cups of water to it, to create 3 cups of liquid **

Black Pudding

1 cup of long grain rice
2 small or 1 large beef bouillon
½ cup of married man's pork (basil substitutes well)
4-5 large wiri wiri peppers or ½ large habernero pepper
1 medium yellow onion mined finely
4 tbsps vegetable oil
3 -4 yards of runners (casing)

2 cups of coconut milk
½ cup fresh thyme leaves
½ cup of African thyme (aka broad leaf thyme)
4 blades of scallion chopped
1 tsp fine salt
1 pint of fresh cows blood

Method:

Wash casings with lime, cut into 12 inch lengths and set aside

Do not let the lime juice sit on casings it changes the texture

Rinse casings thoroughly by filling the interior with water under the tap

Grind thyme leaves, married man's pork or basil, African thyme,

Wiri Wiri peppers, and scallion to a fine paste

Transfer half of this paste to a dish and set aside

In a deep pot, add 2 tbsp of vegetable oil and heat

Saute onion until translucent, but do not brown

Rinse and drain rice and add to pot

Add coconut milk, black pepper, salt, bouillon, and half of seasoning paste

Bring to a boil, reduce, cover, and cook for 20 minutes

Transfer to a large oblong Pyrex or any large deep dish to cool quickly

Add the reserved seasoning paste, and strain the blood directly onto the rice and mix

Bring a large pot filled half filled with water to a boil

Using a wide mouth funnel about 2- 3 inches in circumference

Secure runner (casing) onto mouth of funnel over rice mixture

Spoon mixture into funnel

Use the handle of a wooden spoon to force rice into the casing

Fill casing leaving an inch or so for adjustments

Remove the casing from the funnel

Push mixture from both ends to compress and release any air pockets

If there is more than 2 inches of unfilled casings, use a spoon to add more to fill

But leave at least an inch and a half

Place this sausage in the pot of boiling water

Do not tie the ends of casing, the hot water will shrink it to a close position

Cook for 15 minutes, carefully remove with 2 tongs

Place on a platter and brush lightly with oil

Slice into 2 inch pieces and serve with mango sour condiment (recipe in index)

Slice into 2 inch pieces and serve with **mango sour condiment** (recipe in index)

guyana's tasty exotic

Blueberry Pie with a Pineapple Twist

Pie Crust (check index)
1 cup of fresh pineapple chunks
1/8 tsp. salt
4 tsps. corn starch
1 tbsp. fresh grated ginger
2 tbsp. butter chopped in pieces

4 cups of fresh blueberries
1 cup of light brown sugar
½ tsp. ground cinnamon
1 tbsp. lemon zest
1 tbsp. lemon juice

Reserve for Pie top
1 egg beaten
1 tbsp of light brown sugar reserved for topping

Instructions:
Cut dough in two pieces

Roll out on a floured board

Place one piece in a greased 9" pie dish

Mix the above ingredients except the reserve topping

Transfer into pie dish and spread out evenly

Place the other rolled out pie dough on the top

Cut of overlapping piece of pie dough, leaving 2 inches

Fold and crimp the overlapping dough to create a scalloped edge

Cut four vertical slits in the center of the pie

Brush with a beaten egg

Sprinkle with 1 tbsp. of light brown sugar

Bake for 1 hour until bubbling and brown

Let this pie rest for 20 minutes before serving

Garnish with fresh mint

** In lieu of blueberries, you can use Jamoons if it is available to you, or any other substitute of your choice

Traditionally in my home, Cook-up Rice was a Saturday meal in Guyana. It was generally served with a peppery cucumber salad, and fried fish. Sometimes a beef stew, or some fried chicken worked as a fantastic side. I really enjoy this as is with no side, except for the cucumber salad. I recommend a glass of icy cold swank (home made lemonade) to complete this meal.

Callaloo Cook-Up

1 lb or bunch of spinach or callaloo
1 cup of pumpkin peeled, seeded, and cut into 2 inch pieces
10-12 okras, ends cut off and snipped half
1 cup of coconut milk
1 cup of rice
1 1/4 cup of water
1 ½ tspns of salt
1 tbsp of dried thyme crumbled, or fresh thyme chopped
1 medium yellow onion minced finely
1-2 wiri peppers chopped (optional)
½ tsp freshly ground black pepper
2 tbsp of vegetable or olive oil
2 blades of finely chopped scallion/ eschalot

Method:
In a large pot, saute onion for 2 minutes on medium heat

Add all ingredients, except spinach/callaloo, and scallion

Bring to a rapid boil and reduce heat low to simmer and cover

Cook for 15 minutes, then remove cover from sauce pot and

Add spinach/callaloo

Do not stir, cover and cook for an additional five minutes

Remove lid and stir

Transfer to a serving platter and top with scallions

Serve hot

Chinese food in Guyana is very memorable to many. The aroma that fills the air when you walk by one of these restaurants is their advertisement for delicious foods. Just seeing the roast meats hanging from the glass window of a restaurant as you go by, or hearing the sizzle of foods being prepared in a wok is enough to make you order a mixed Lo-mein, Fried Rice, roast pork, and Chop Suey to go....

Canton Char Sui/Cantonese Barbeque Pork Belly

- 3 lbs pork belly or pork shoulder
- 2 tbsp fresh ground ginger
- 3 tbsp yellow bean sauce (brown bean sauce)
- 5 cloves of garlic grounded
- 5 tbsp sugar
- 5 tbsp dark soy sauce
- 2 tbsp Shoishing wine or sherry
- 1/3 cup honey
- 2 tbsp five spice powder
- 1 tsp sesame paste
- 1 tbsp vegetable oil
- 2 tbsp oyster sauce
- 1 tsp bright red coloring (optional)

Method:

Add all ingredients except pork to a bowl and mix thoroughly

Place in a clear plastic or ziplock bag and refrigerate overnight

Remove and rest on a wire rack placed in a baking pan for 45 minutes

Pre heat oven to 400 degrees

Roast for 20 minutes

Reduce oven temperature to 300 degrees and roast for 30 minutes

While baking baste all marinade with a brush onto meat

Remove from oven and rest for 10 minutes

Slice pork thinly, served with steamed rice and steamed Chinese vegetables

Caribbean BBQ Sauce

- 2 cups of ketchup
- 2 tbsp tomato paste
- 1 medium yellow onion minced
- 3 cloves of garlic minced
- 1 tsp chilli powder
- 1 tsp allspice
- 3 tbsp molasses
- ½ tsp ground coriander
- 1 tsp cumin
- ½ tsp salt
- 4 tbsp brown sugar
- 1 cup tamarind pulp
- 1 tbsp horseradish
- 1 tbsp vegetable oil
- 1 cup water

Method:

Saute onions in a sauce pot until translucent

Add garlic and saute for 1 minute

Toss in chilli powder, allspice, coriander, cumin, and salt

Stir and saute for a minute

Add all other ingredients and bring to a boil

Reduce and simmer for 30 minutes

Store in a jar in the refrigerator for up to 2 months

Use this to brush on grilled shrimps, fish, chicken or steaks

Caribbean Pineapple Holiday Ham

1 bone in pork leg
4 tbsp fresh thyme minced finely
2 tbsp soy sauce
2 tbsp olive oil
1/4 cup brown sugar
1/4 cup of whole cloves

1 head of garlic peeled and grounded
3 tbsp Dijon mustard
1 tbsp sea salt
½ cup maple syrup
1 fresh pineapple, peeled, cored, and sliced into rings

Method:

Score the skin of the ham in a diamond pattern

Do not cut through to meat

Combine thyme, garlic, mustard, soy, maple syrup, olive oil, and brown sugar to make a marinade

Pour and rub generously using up all of the marinade

Cover tightly and refrigerate overnight

Remove one hour prior to roasting before placing in the oven

This is to temper ham to make ready for the oven

Place pineapple rounds strategically around ham

Secure pineapple rings with toothpicks

Preheat oven to 325 degrees

Place a meat thermometer in the thickest part of ham

Cover loosely with aluminum foil and place in the middle rack of the oven

Roast for 6 hours, remove foil in the last half hour of cooking

Remove from oven to counter top

Rest for 30 minutes before carving

To ensure proper cooking thermometer must register a minimum of 160 degrees

Caribbean Pineapple Holiday Ham

Caribbean She-Crab Soup

1 lb of lump crab meat
3 cups of freshly shucked roasted corn
5 cups of shrimp stock or chicken stock
3 limes (rolled to soften, zested & juiced)
½ tbsp Adobo Seasoning Salt (optional)
½ white onion finely minced (Vidalia is preferred)
2 fire roasted chipolte peppers (minced)
1 roasted jalapeno (seeded and minced)
1 avocado diced
½ cup of diced sweet mango
1/3 cup finely minced cilantro
1/4 tsp. of sea salt
1/4 tsp. white pepper
½ tsp. lightly toasted cumin seeds
1/4 cup of soft white breadcrumbs
tortilla chips garnishing

Method:
Combine lime juice, zest, roasted corn,

Adobo seasoning salt, shrimp or chicken stock, salt,

pepper, roasted jalapeno, onions, white bread crumbs in a blender and pulse for 2 minutes into form a rustic soup broth.

Ladle Soup Broth into six bowls.

Layer crab meat, avocado, and mango in that order onto the broth.

Top with crumbled tortilla chips, lightly toasted cumin seeds, and cilantro.

Serve immediately with a twist of lime.

Caribe Banana Muffins

1 cup of whole wheat flour
1 cup of all purpose flour
1 cup brown sugar
½ cup melted butter
1 tbsp cinnamon
3 ripe bananas mashed
2 eggs beaten
1 tbsp vanilla essence
3/4 cup of milk
1/4 cup of grounded flax seeds
1 tsp ground allspice
1 tsp baking soda
1 tsp baking powder
½ tsp salt
4 dates or figs finely chopped

Method:
Heat oven to 375 degrees

Sift all the dry ingredients together in a large bowl

Mash bananas, add milk, melted butter and vanilla and mix well

Combine with dry ingredients

Grease muffin pans

Pour into muffin pans and bake for 15-20 minutes

If making a banana bread, pour into a loaf pan

Bake this for 40 - 45 minute

Use a toothpick inserted in the center to see if this is cooked

guyana's tasty exotic

I met Chan at a wake house of a mutual friend of ours. As I was leaving, she had just arrived with loads of prepared foods. My friend insisted that I try her Cassava Pone, after I happily complied, I was solidly hooked. I gathered a few pieces and made myself a care package to go. As I headed for my car, I turned back to inquire if she'd be so inclined to share her recipe with me for my book. She was delighted and flattered. We became fast friends, and we actually tested this recipe together in my very own kitchen. It is awesome, I promise!

Chan Jairam's Cassava Pone

5 lbs cassava peeled and grated
or equal to 6 cups
1 coconut grated finely
or equal 2 ½ cups
3 cups of light brown sugar
1 cup of golden raisins
1 tbspn vanilla
4 tbspns butter
1 tspn freshly grated nutmeg
1 tspn black pepper freshly grated
1 cup hot water

Method:
Heat oven to 350 degrees

Grease a 9" x 12" Pyrex or baking pan generously with butter

Bring 1 cup of water to a boil

Mix all ingredients well, except water

After incorporating ingredients well

Add hot water, (this activates the starch,

and give the end product a nice sticky finish)

Mix well, pour into buttered pyrex/pan

Dot with little pieces of butter throughout the top

Bake for 75 minutes or until golden brown

Cool for 30 minutes before cutting into squares

** Cassava is also known as Yuca

Pineapple Rum Chicken ala Caribbean

2 boneless, skinless chicken breasts split into 4 pieces
4 -6 round slices of fresh pineapple
2 tbsp brown sugar
2 tablespoons lime juice
1/4 cup Caribbean rum or a good substitute
2 tbsp molasses
1 tbsp vegetable oil
1/4 tsp white pepper
1/4 tsp salt
1 tsp. five spice powder
2 tbsp chopped shallots
1 cup of chicken stock
2 tbsp. finely chopped chives or green onion

Instructions:
Caramelize pineapple in brown sugar, lime juice,

molasses, and brown sugar.

Cook for 2 minutes on both sides, and set aside.

Season chicken with salt, pepper, and five spice powder.

Sear on medium heat for 4-5 minutes on each side.

Remove chicken and set aside.

Saute shallots in pan drippings for 2 minutes.

Return chicken to pan and add rum.

Continue to cook on high heat until rum is absorbed

Place caramelized pineapple slices on top of chicken

Add chicken stock, reduce heat to medium, and cover

Cook for 5-8 minutes or until most of the

liquid has been reduced to a thick consistency.

Transfer chicken to a serving platter, and spoon pan juices on top.

Sprinkle with green onions (scallions) or chives.

Serve with a side of root vegetables or a vegetable pilaf.

Cheese Rolls

Pastry dough (see index for recipe)
1 lb of finely grated sharp cheddar cheese
1/4 lb butter (softened at room temp)
2 tbsp French mustard
1/4 cup chopped chives or minced scallions
1 tbsp of finely ground hot peppers (such as wiri wiri, red bonnet, or chilies)
1 egg beaten with 1 tbsp of milk

Method:
Section pastry into 4 parts

In a large mixing bowl combine everything except dough and egg mixture

Roll out pastry dough, and use a circular cookie cutter to cut 4"disks

Use a pastry brush to bate egg wash on the circumference of disk

Spread 1 tbsp of cheese mixture on dough and roll sides to overlap each other

Press with fingers to seal ends

Use a fork to further seal and design edges to neatness

Prick top with egg mixture

Place on a greased baking sheet or wax paper

Bake for 15-20 minutes

Place on a wire rack for 10 minutes before serving

A recipe for Cheese Straws the way it is made in the Caribbean. Everything in the Caribbean is hot, which is what makes it so good as we all know.

Cheese Straws

1 lb flour
3/4 lbs butter
3/4 lbs grated sharp cheddar
½ tspn Coleman's dry mustard
or 1 teaspoon of French's Mustard(prepared)
½ tspn white pepper
3 wiri peppers chopped finely/grounded
or ½ scotch bonnet pepper finely grounded
1 egg yolk
1 tbspn cold whole milk
½ tspn baking soda

Method:
Heat oven to 375 degrees

Using a pastry chopper, dice butter in small pieces

combine flour, baking soda, cheese, white pepper,

hot pepper, and mustard

Beat egg yolk with milk and pour into flour mixture

binding to form a ball

Refrigerate for 30 min

Roll out onto a floured board into 1/4 inch thickness

Cut into drinking straw size lengths or of desired size

Bake for 8-10 minutes

Cool before serving as they can crumble if handled hot

Carifest 2009 Celebration

guyana's tasty exotic

Chicken Biryani

1 whole chicken cut into 16 pieces
4 green cardamoms
1/4 cup chopped cilantro
1 tbsp of fresh grated ginger
1 tsp brown cumin
1 ½ cups of plain yogurt
4 whole cloves
1 tsp lime juice
2 curry leaves
2 green chilies minced
4 cloves of garlic minced
2 tbsp vegetable oil

2 cups Basmati rice (pre soaked for 30 minutes)
2 black cardamoms
2 tbsp chopped mint
1 tsp of whole black cumin
1 large yellow onion (sliced thinly)
1 cinnamon stick (3" long)
1 tsp mace
2 bay leaves
1 tbsp turmeric
½ tsp saffron threads
2 ½ tsp salt

Method:

Bring 3 ½ cups of water to a boil and add 1 tsp of salt

Transfer rice to pot and bring to a boil

Stir contiguously and cook until rice has a slight grain

Set aside In a bowl, mix green and black cardamom, cilantro, mint, ginger, brown and black cumin, cinnamon, cloves, mace, lime juice, bay leaves, curry leaves, turmeric, chilies, saffron threads, garlic, yogurt, and 1 ½ tsp salt to form a paste

Wash and pat chicken pieces dry

Add spice mixture to meat

In a heavy bottom pot add oil and heat

Add onion and fry until crispy and slightly brown

Reserve oil and set fried onions aside

Add chicken to oil and saute on high heat for 15 minutes

Add rice to chicken and cover with a tight lid

Cook on high heat for 5 minutes and reduce heat to medium flame

Cook for 15 minutes

Keeping lid on at all times

Cook for an additional 10 minutes on low heat

Remove lid and carefully stir

Top with fried onions and sprigs of cilantro

Chickens in the countryside

guyana's tasty exotic

Ashley Ro Hall, her boyfriend Tyronne, Mom Monique, along with her Uncle Malcom Hall really cleaned their plates when I fixed them this meal. Here is a photo of the actual Lo-Mein that was prepared upon their visit. I hope it brings them great food memories.

Chicken Lo Mein

1 (4) lb chicken cut into 16 pieces
1 tbsp freshly grated ginger
1 tbsp cornstarch
1 tbsp hoisin sauce
1 tbsp sesame oil
3 tbsp Chinese rice wine
2 tbsp soy sauce
1 tsp white pepper
1 tbsp garlic paste
1 tsp five spice powder

Wash and pat chicken pieces until dry, and set aside
In a bowl mix all other ingredients well
Combine this mixture with the chicken pieces

1 lb of Chinese noodles
½ lb of bora (Chinese long bean) cut in 2" pieces
2 medium carrots sliced into thin rounds
3 bunches of Chinese greens, chopped coarsely
1 cup of finely shredded cabbage
3 tbsp soy sauce
2 chicken bouillons
½ tsp white pepper
6 blades of finely sliced scallion
1 large white onion chopped
3 wiri wiri peppers minced(optional)
5 tbsp vegetable oil
1/4 cup of water
½ tsp five spice powder

Chicken Lo Mein

Method:
Boil, cook, and drain noodles
Set aside
In a wok, add 3 tbsp vegetable oil
Heat on a high flame, add chicken pieces
Cook until all liquid is absorbed and chicken is browned
Remove chicken and set aside
Add 2 tbsp vegetable oil to the wok
Toss in onions, bora, and carrots and cook for 2 minutes on high heat
Add bouillions and water and continue to cook until water is almost absorbed
Add cabbage, wiri wiri pepper, and Chinese greens, and cook for 1 minute
Return chicken to pot, and add noodles, soy sauce, and white pepper, and five spice powder
Mix well and top with chopped scallions

guyana's tasty exotic

A favorite in my household, this soup made it's television debut on the Dr. Oz show in February, 2010. It was shown in a segment called "Natural Home Remedies", and won in a competition against two other types of home remedies. Dr. Oz declared it's medicinal value, citing that it does indeed help to cure the common cold. This recipe can also be found in the Dr. Oz show recipe archive.

Chicken Soup (a.k.a. Jewish Penicillin)

1 (4) lb. chicken cut into quarters pieces
3 long celery stalks (cut into halves)
6 black peppercorns
1 bunch of fresh dill
1 ½ tbsp kosher salt or coarse sea salt
3 turnips peeled and cut into quarters
½ tsp white pepper

6 medium sized carrots peeled and cut into 2"
2 large yellow onions quartered
1 bunch of parsley
6 Turkish bay leaves
3 tbsp butter
3 parsnips peeled and cut into 2" pieces
2 ½ quarts of water

Method:

Wash and prepare all vegetables, and set aside

Reserve 6 sprigs of dill and chop finely, and set aside

Reserve 4 sprigs of parsley and chop finely, and set aside

Tie together, the remainder of parsley and dill with butchers twine

Wash and pat chicken dry with paper towels

Sprinkle with ½ tsp of salt and the white pepper on both sides

In a Dutch oven or a heavy bottomed soup pot, add 2 tbsp of butter

Heat on a high flame and place chicken skin side up and sear until brown

This should take about 2-3 minutes

Flip chicken pieces and do the same to brown

Add water and layer with bay leaves, peppercorns, onions, carrots, celery,

turnips, parsnips, and the remainder of salt

Bring this to a rapid boil, place the tied parsley and dill in the pot

Add the remainder of butter(1tbsp) to soup if a white foam appears

This is a little trick to help it to dissipate, in order to achieve a clear broth

Reduce heat to a medium simmer and cook for 1 hour

Using a slotted spoon, remover dill and parsley bunch and discard

Remove parsnips, turnips, bay leaves, peppercorns, onions, and celery and discard

Remove skin form chicken and discard

Transfer chicken pieces to a soup tureen, and then carrots

Finally skim fat from broth and pour in the soup tureen,

Top with fresh chopped dill and parsley

Cover to keep warm

If you are making Matzo balls or noodles, after carrots and chicken have been removed from soup, cook them in this broth to intensify their flavor. Add matzo balls to the tureen, and carefully pour broth to top, top with fresh chopped dill and parsley.

Pot of Chicken Soup

Matzo Balls My Way

1 cup of matzo meal
1/8 tsp white pepper
4 tbsp vegetable oil
4 tbsp fresh dill chopped

1 tsp fine salt
4 eggs
6 tbsp chicken broth
1 tsp baking powder

Method:

In a mixing bowl add matzo and baking powder, mix well, and set aside

Whisk eggs, salt, white pepper, dill, chicken stock, and vegetable oil

Pour this into the matzo meal mixture and combine well

Do not be deterred by its soggy appearance

Cover and refrigerate for 30 minutes

Bring soup stock to a boil

Fill a small bowl with water for wetting hands

Remove mixture from refrigerator, wet hands and mold into tennis balls size

Add to pot of water or stock, they will pop up to the top

Cover and simmer on low for 25 minutes, be sure to flip them in while cooking

Let them rest in soup stock to expand and absorb broth for 20 minutes before serving

Ladle in a soup bowls and serve

Chocolate Chip Scones

2 cups all purpose flour
1/3 cup white sugar
1 ½ tsp baking powder
1/8 tsp salt
8 tbsp (1 stick) unsalted butter
1 cup chocolate chips
1 tbsp vanilla extract
1 cup buttermilk
1 egg beaten

Directions:
Preheat oven to 375 degrees

Add to a mixing bowl, flour, sugar, baking powder, and salt

Add cold butter and emulsify to a crumbly mixture

Add chocolate chips and stir in

Whisk buttermilk, vanilla, and egg together and add to flour mixture

Knead very lightly into dough to form a ball

Knead dough onto a lightly floured surface

Roll out into a circle about 2" thick

Cut into triangles using a pastry cutter

Place onto a greased pan and brush with egg wash

Bake for about 20 minutes or until golden brown

Egg Wash:
1 egg
1 tbsp milk
1/4 tsp vanilla

Beat together and brush generously on scones before baking

Coriander and Mint chutney

1 cup of fresh coriander leaves
½ cup mint leaves
2-3 green chillies
½ tsp salt
1/4 teaspoon sugar
1 teaspoon lemon juice

Method:
Place mint, green chillies and coriander in a food processor and grind or pound in a mortar and pestle

Transfer to a bowl, and add the other ingredients

Mix well and rest for 20 minutes

Serve with appetizers as a condiment

Cornish Pasty originated from Cornwall, England. It was made specially for the miners of Cornwall's Mining Industry by their loving wives for hundreds of years. When many miners migrated to other countries, they continued making Cornish Pasties which can be found in many other places other than Cornwall.

Cornish Pasties

Dough

1 ½ cups all purpose flour
8 tbsp butter
6 tbsp of iced water

½ tsp baking powder
3/4 tsp salt

Method:
Sift all dry ingredients in a bowl

Add butter and emulsify into sifted ingredients

Slowly add iced water until formed into a ball

Cover and refrigerate for 30 minutes before using

Filling
Combine all the above ingredients and set aside

Ingredients:
1 lb lamb or chuck steak (cut into small cubes)
1 large potato diced (approx. 1 cup)
1 large carrot diced (approx. ½ cup)
1 large yellow onion minced
1 turnip diced (approx. 1/3 cup)
2 tbsp finely chopped parsley
1 tsp salt
½ tsp ground black pepper
2 tbsp Worcestershire sauce
2 tbsp of fresh chopped thyme

Pre heat over to 375 degrees

Cut dough into 4 pieces and roll out into 1/4" thick circles

Place a 1/4 of filling into the center

Fold in half and roll edges overlapping by 1/2", pinching to seal

Cut a 1" cris cross slit to allow steam to escape during baking

Brush with egg wash (1 egg + 1 tbsp water whisked together)

Bake for 40 minutes or until golden brown

Cornish Pasty

A British recipe jazzed up to my standards, this recipe can be made ahead and be reheated in the oven before serving. Definitely have this with a side salad or a side of steamed mixed vegetables.

Cottage Pie

1 lb of chopped meat
1 pack frozen peas and carrots
1 large onion finely chopped
2 cloves of garlic minced
2 tbsp all purpose flour
2 tbsp butter
2 tbsp vegetable oil
2 beef bouillon
1 tsp Worcestershire sauce
2 tbsp tomato paste
1 tbsp horseradish
2 cups boiling water
2 cups of hot beef stock
1 tsp salt
1 tsp ground black pepper
1 tsp ground allspice

Topping
4 cups of mashed potatoes
1 tbsp of chopped thyme
1 tbsp chopped parsley
1 tbsp butter
1/4 cup of milk
1 tsp salt
½ tsp ground black pepper

Method:
In a heavy bottomed pot, saute onion and garlic for 2 minutes

Add ground beef and brown slightly

Add Worcestershire sauce, tomato paste, horse radish, bouillon,

allspice, salt, and pepper, and cook for 1 minute

Add vegetables, beef stock and water

Cook on high heat for 20 minutes

Combine flour and butter to form a roux

Place roux in the bubbling meat sauce and stir in well

After gravy is thicken, transfer to a pyrex

Method:
Saute thyme and parsley

Add all other ingredients to potatoes and mix well

Place this on top of meat mixture and smooth with a spatula

Bake in a 400 degree oven for 45 minutes or until bubbling and golden brown

Cows grazing in Guyana

If this sounds un-palatable, substitute with pieces of beef or pork. A gelatinous Saturday afternoon specialty of pickled meat, it is not unusual to see a lady go from house to house selling Souse and Black Pudding on a Friday and Saturday afternoon. As a matter of fact, it has been a downright Guyanese tradition since I can remember, and one that is always lucrative to the vendor.

Cow feet Souse

2 medium sized calf feet cut into 4" pieces
1 lb cheeks of a calf (skin only)
2 ½ tbsp of salt
4 limes (3 juiced, 1 cut in half)
1 large cucumber (de-seeded and sliced thinly)
1 medium white onion minced finely
3 large wiri peppers OR 1 scotch bonnet pepper minced
2 blades of finely diced scallion
2 - 3 sprigs of parsley
1 sprig of celery leaves minced
½ cup of white distilled vinegar
6-8 cups of water

Method:
Clean meat with 1 lime, and rinse well
In a large stock pot place meat and fill with water
Make sure water is covering meat about six inches higher than where meat sits in the pot
Bring to a rapid boil, add 2 tbsp salt and reduce heat
to simmer
Cover and cook slowly for about 1 ½ - 2 hours or until meat is fork tender
Strain and reserve liquid, and set meat aside
Allow meat and broth to come to room temperature
In a large bowl, combine peppers, onion, cucumbers, celery, parsley,
salt, lime juice, and vinegar
Let this rest for 10 minutes
Stir constantly to induce water extraction from cucumbers and onions
Pour stock and mix well
Add meat pieces carefully
Spoon marinade generously over meat to infuse flavors of seasonings
Let this rest at room temp for 30 minutes to marinate before serving
Serve with wedges of lime and ice cold beer.

Creolese Grilled Shrimp

18 large Shrimp
2 limes juice and zested
4 tbsp low sodium soy sauce
3 tbsp of fresh thyme leaves
3 large garlic cloves
1 scotch bonnet or 2 large wiri wiri peppers
1/4 cup of light olive oil
2 tbsp of Dijon mustard
½ tsp white pepper
2 tbsp tamarind pulp
1 tbsp grated ginger

Method:
Clean and remove vein from shrimp

Leave a small piece of tail at the end

In a food processor or using a motor and pestle combine garlic,

thyme and scotch bonnet pepper and grind to a paste

Add lime juice, zest, tamarind pulp, soy sauce, mustard,

white pepper, ginger, and olive oil

Combine well

Reserve 3 tablespoon of marinade for dressing

Pour the remainder onto shrimp

Refrigerate for 1-2 hours for optimum flavor

Thread onto a bamboo or metal skewers

Grill for three minutes on each side

Remove and brush with additional marinade

In Guyana, Sundays were never the same if you weren't having Curried chicken with Rice, Dhal, and a side of Chowmein in my home. Going to the market, selecting your bird, having it slaughtered, then roasting off the left over feathers on an open fire, intensified the flavors of your chicken, which was customary, and made your meals flavourful and tasty in a unique way..

Curried Chicken With Potatoes

1 whole chicken (4-5lbs) cut into16 pieces
3 medium sized potatoes
1 large tomato
1 medium onion
4 large cloves of garlic
½ cup of chopped cilantro(optional)
2 tsp garam masala
1 ½ tbsp of curry powder
1 ½ tsp salt
3 whole cloves
4 cardamom pods
2 elaichi pods
1 cinnamon stick (approx.3")
1 tbsp of fresh ground ginger
1-2 green chilies or 2 wiri wiri peppers
2 cups of chicken stock or water
2 tbsp of vegetable oil

Curried Chicken

Method:
Wash chicken pieces and pat dry

Add salt, cloves, and cinnamon stick to meat

Pour oil in a deep skillet or a cast iron pot

Heat oil at high heat, after it has been heated

Reduce to medium and saute meat

Cook until liquid spewed from meat has been absorbed

Meantime, grind onion, tomato, peppers, garlic and cilantro

Mix well with curry powder, garam masala and ginger

Form this mixture into a paste

Add paste to chicken

Wash, scrub and cut potatoes into quarters (3" pieces)

Saute marinated chicken for about 3 minutes

Add potatoes and continue to saute on medium to low heat

Saute this for another 3 minutes

Add hot chicken stock or hot water

Bring to a rapid boil, and cover

Reduce heat to a medium to low simmer and cook for 20 minutes

Or until liquid must reduce to a thick gravy and potatoes are fork tender

Top with some chopped cilantro (optional)

guyana's tasty exotic

Curried Goat Caribbean style is very popular here in the States. I know that many people associate this meal with Jamaica, but this is quite a common dish in Guyana. This recipe works well if you want to make Curried Beef, or Venison Curried as well.

Caribbean Goat Curry

3 lbs of goat meat with bones
4 garlic cloves minced
1 medium onion finely minced
2 blades of scallion minced
2 tbsp Madras curry powder
1/4 tsp ground cloves
1 cinnamon stick
1 beef bouillon
3 cups of boiling hot water

3 medium sized tomatoes finely chopped
1/4 cup of finely chopped coriander
1 scotch bonnet pepper minced
1 lime juiced
1 tsp ground cumin
½ tsp ground allspice
½ tsp salt
1 tbsp vegetable oil

Method:

Wash goat meat pieces well, and drain.

Pour lime juice and skins on meat

Rinse meat well and discard lime skins

Drain well place in a bowl

Add curry powder, ground cumin, onion, allspice, cloves, coriander

Scotch bonnet pepper, salt, and 1 tbsp of Madras curry powder to meat

Mix well and cover tightly

Refrigerate for an hour or overnight

Before cooking, remove from refrigerator and let it sit for 30 minutes

Heat oil in a pot

Place marinated goat meat and saute

Cook until all liquid is absorbed and slightly browned

Add tomatoes and continue to cook for two minutes

Add curry powder, bouillon, and continue to saute on medium heat

Add water, and bring to rapid boil

Reduce and simmer for 2 hours until gravy is thick and meat is tender

Transfer to a serving platter and sprinkle with Scallions

Serve with Peas and Rice or Roti

Dhal Puri

Filling
1 cup yellow split peas
1 tsp salt
1 tsp ground geera (cumin)
3 cloves of garlic
2 hot red pepper(wiri wiri)
2 blades of scallion

Method:
Boil split peas until cooked about 20 minutes

Check for doneness by pressing a

pea on a hard surface

If it collapses to a fine mash that

isn't mushy

It is good to go, strain and grind using a

rolling pin or food processor

Be careful not to over cook this, because

it can become too soft

Grind garlic, pepper, and scallion to a paste

Add this paste, along with geera (cumin)

to grounded split peas

Mix well, and set aside

Dough for Dhal Puri
4 cups all purpose flour
1 tsp baking powder
½ tsp salt
2 tbsp vegetable oil
1 ½ - 2 cups warm water to make a dough

Method:
Sift all dry ingredients

Drizzle oil and mix

Add water in increments of half cups

Bind into a firm but soft dough

Use 1 tsp of oil to moisten dough

Spread it lightly with fingers

This will keep dough moist and soft

And eliminate any hard skin that might form

Cover with a kitchen towel

Let this rest for 30 minutes

Cut dough into 8 pieces

Flatten into a small flat round about 3-4 inches in diameter

Place 2 ½ tbsp of ground split pea mixture

Pull ends together and pinch into a tight seal

Press into a bit of flour and set aside

Let this rest for about 20-30 minutes

To cook Dhal puri:
Heat a flat non-stick pan or a Tawa

Place some oil in a bowl with a culinary paint brush

Light brush some oil on the heated pan

Roll out filled dough very carefully, dusting with flour lightly

Use your rolling pin to roll in a swivel method

This will distribute the filling evenly

Place on the hot pan, and 30 seconds flip with a spatula

Brush oil onto surface of Dhal Puri

Flip and lightly brush the other side

Bake time is approximately 30 -40 seconds on each side

Remove and place on a platter

Cook and stack these on top of each other

Best served with your favorite curry

Dumplings

1 cup flour
½ tsp baking powder
½ tsp salt
2 tbsp sugar
1 cup water
2 tbsp butter

Method:

Combine all ingredients to make dough soft

Add more or less water upon desecration if needed

Spoon about 1 tbsp into Soup or Metemgee

Cover pot to cook for 8 minutes

To cook in water do the same and remove promptly after 8 minutes

Place in a Pyrex and cover to retain softness

Dumplings can also be served with a robust beef stew

* For Soup and Metemgee recipe refer to index

Eggnog

16 oz Bourbon
2 cup of cream
3 cups milk
2 tbsp vanilla extract OR
1 split vanilla bean
1 tsp freshly grated nutmeg
6 egg yolks
½ cup white sugar
1 tsp almond extract

Method:

Combine milk and vanilla and bring to a boil

Remove from heat and set aside

In a bowl whisk egg yolks, sugar, and cream

Slowly add egg mixture to hot milk and continue to whisk

Return to stove and cook on medium heat stirring continuously

Add almond extract and nutmeg

Continue to whisk until thickened

Remove from stove, add Bourbon and stir well

Pour into a pitcher and refrigerate to chill

Serve, topped with extra grated nutmeg

Fish Cakes always work great as an accompaniment to Cook-up Rice. It is also terrific on bread, and can also be served as an appetizer. Here in the US, Americans enjoy their fish cakes with spaghetti. This is the way I was taught to make them. And while I make this in several other methods, this one remains my ultimate favorite.

Fish Cakes

1 lb of white fish (Trout or any mild white fish)
1/3 cup mashed potatoes
1 tablespoon chopped parsley
2-3 wiri wiri pepper or ½ scotch bonnet minced finely
½ tsp salt
1 tbsp lime juice
2 eggs whisked

1 bay leaf
1 tablespoon of melted butter
½ medium onion grated finely
2 tbsp finely chopped thyme
½ tsp ground white pepper
1/8 tsp Worcestershire sauce (substitute- soy sauce)
½ cup canola or vegetable oil

Seasoned Bread Crumbs for coating
1/3 cup of dried bread crumbs
1 /2 tsp white pepper
1 tbsp chopped parsley
1 tsp paprika

Combine these ingredients and set aside for coating fish patties
If you prefer to use pre-seasoned bread crumbs, there is no need to season your coating

Method:
Cut fish in small pieces(about 4 inches)
Place bay leaf in a pot add 1 cup of water
Bring to a boil to infuse flavor
Reduce to a low simmer, add fish pieces, and cover
Steam for 4 -5 minutes
Drain and cool fish pieces, and discard bay leaf
Remove all skin and bones from fish

Place fish pieces in a mixing bowl
Add potatoes, melted butter, parsley, onion, wiri wiri pepper, salt, lemon juice, thyme worcheshire sauce, white pepper, and 1 egg
Bind these ingredients together working them into a nice mold

Use an ice cream scoop to measure equal amounts
Press and shape into patties
Dip in whisked egg wash and then dried breadcrumbs
Pan fry using a non-stick pan on medium heat until golden brown

African Guyanese Dancers Independence Day 2009

Fish Masala

1 tbsp ground turmeric
1 tbsp cumin seeds
1 tbsp mustard seeds
1 tbsp mangrile seeds
1 tbsp coriander seeds
½ tbsp black pepper corns
6 dried red chillies
8 curry leaves

Method:
In a hot skillet and on medium heat, parch mustard seeds, cumin seeds,

and coriander seeds until they appear to be jumping out of the pot

Add red chillies, curry leaves, and mustard seeds and parch for 30 seconds

Stir continuously while these are parching, to avoid burning

Transfer to a mortar and pestle, or a coffee grinder

Grind to a powder from

Store in a jar for seafood curries or other seafood recipes requiring masala

Fish Pie with Cheese

Pastry Dough Rolled out for a 9" deep dish
2 medium ripe tomatoes
1 lb steam white fish (flaked Haddock)
2 tbsp chopped parsley
1 tsp capers
1 tbsp butter
3/4 cup milk
1 tbsp lemon juice
½ tsp white pepper
½ tsp salt
2 tbsp flour
1 cup grated cheddar cheese
1 tsp thyme

Method:
Preheat oven to 375 degrees

Place fish in a sauce pot with milk, thyme, salt and pepper

Bring to a boil

Add butter in the pan

Mix butter and flour into a round firm ball

Add ½ cup of cheese

Simmer until it thickens

Pour into Pyrex

Place tomato slices on top to cover mixture

Sprinkle the remainder of cheddar and bake in the oven for 30 minutes

What exactly is Foo Foo? It is an African side dish. It is quite simple to prepare, using a mortar and pestle. A side of Foo Foo can be served with a robust Beef Stew. Additionally this can be added to a bowl of soup to create a hearty meal.

Foo Foo

1 lb or 3 green plantains
1 ½ tsp of salt
½ tsp of grounded black pepper
4 tbsp of butter/vegetable oil

Method:

Peel plantains and cut into 2" pieces

Place into a deep pot with and add salt

Add enough water to cover plantains about 2" over

Cook on medium heat until fork tender about 20 minutes

Drain and reserve about a cup of liquid from the pot

Add butter and pepper to hot drained plantains

Using a mortar and pestle, pound plantains while they are still hot

Add small amounts of reserved liquid to achieve a smooth paste

Pound until there aren't any lumps

Remove mixture and dampen hands with water

Mold into size of cricket balls or desired size

Place Foo Foo balls in a Pyrex and cover to keep moist and warm or until ready to serve with stew or soup of your choice

Fooncee

2 Chinese eggplants
2 ozs of rice noodles
2 lbs of chicken breast (sliced thinly)
2 ozs of tiger lily mushrooms
(also known as bat ears)
2 cloves of garlic minced
3 blades of scallions thinly sliced
1 medium onion minced
2 tsp minced ginger
2 tbsp cornstarch
1 cup of chicken stock
1/4 cup of Shoisin rice wine
1 tbsp sesame oil
1 tbsp vegetable oil
½ tsp white pepper
3 tbsp oyster sauce
2 tbsp soy sauce

Method:

Cut eggplant into 1" thick rounds(soak in a bowl of water, and set aside)

Reconstitute rice noodles in water, and set that aside as well

Reconstitute tiger lily mushrooms in cold water, and set aside

Slice chicken into thin slivers, place in a bowl, and add 1 tsp ginger, 1 tbsp cornstarch, Shoisin rice wine, white pepper, 1 tbsp oyster sauce, 1 tbsp soy sauce, and sesame oil

Mix well and set aside

Heat on a 1 tbsp vegetable oil high flame, using a wok or non stick pan

Add chicken and stir constantly for 2 minutes, and remove

Return wok to stove top, add the remainder vegetable oil heat

Toss in onions, garlic, eggplant, ginger, hoisin and soy sauces

Cook this for about 2-3 minutes stirring constantly

Add rice noodles, tiger lily, and chicken stock, cook for 3 minutes covered

Return chicken to wok and cook for 1 minute

Add 2 tbsp of water to 1 tbsp cornstarch and stir well

Add this to the wok and cook for 1 minute or until thickened

Transfer to a serving dish

Sprinkle scallions on top

Serve over steamed jasmine rice

guyana's tasty exotic 33

Savory Fried Okra Fritters

1 lb fresh okra
½ cup cornmeal
½ cup flour
1 tsp. baking powder
1 tsp turmeric
½ tsp ground geera (cumin)
1 tsp garlic minced
½ medium finely minced onion
1 tbsp scotch bonnet pepper minced or any hot pepper
½ tsp ground coriander powder
1 tbsp fresh finely chopped coriander leaves
1 tsp salt
1/4 tsp ground black pepper
1 egg
½ cup warm water
1 cup of vegetable oil

Instructions:

Wash and dry okras, then cut into 2"thick pieces

Combine all ingredients except vegetable oil in a deep mixing bowl

Heat oil on a medium flame

Drop 2 tablespoons of batter into hot pan with oil

Cook for 1 ½ -2 minutes on each side until golden brown

Serve with Mango Sour Condiment (see index for recipe)

Fried Shark

6 pieces of shark steaks (6oz pieces)
6-8 leaves of bandania (optional)
4 cloves of garlic
4 leaves of African thyme (broad leaf thyme)
1 tbsp of English thyme leaves
1 habernero or scotch bonnet pepper
2 limes
1 cup of white distilled vinegar
1 ½ tablespoons of fine salt
1 tsp of black pepper
1 cup of all purpose flour

Method:

Place shark in a large shallow dish, (or any fish off your preference)

Roll limes on hard surface until soften and juice

Pour lime juice and vinegar over fish

Add 1 tbsp of salt and reserve the rest

Add the juice of limes

Letting this sit for ½ hour

Rinse fish and pat dry with a towel

Grind garlic, bandana, hot pepper, and thymes in a food processor

or a mortar and pestle to make a paste

Cut little slits into fish and fill with seasoning paste

Sprinkle with ½ of the black pepper and reserve the rest

Meantime, in a shallow bowl pour flour, add the rest of the black pepper,

and the remaining salt and mix well

Heat oil in a deep skillet on medium heat

Coat fish with flour mixture

Fry until golden brown on both sides

Serve with Bakes and your choice of condiments and or toppings

Garam Masala consist of several spices that have been toasted and grounded to a fine dust to dress either meats or seafood. So it is only fitting that these masalas will be flavored differently to compliment your choice of protein and vegetables. Here is my masala recipe for meat.

Garam Masala for Meat

3 green cardamom pods
1 whole bay leaf
8 whole cloves
1 (3")cinnamon stick (broken into small pieces)
5 tbsp coriander seeds
2 tsp fennel seeds

4 curry leaves
3 elaichi pods (black cardamom)
½ tsp black peppercorns
5 whole dried red chilies
3 tbsp cumin seeds
1 tbsp ground turmeric

Method:
Lightly toast all the spices in a pan, except for curry leaves, bay leaf, dried chili peppers, and ground turmeric.

When the spices are almost done toasting, add curry leaves, bay leaf, and dried chili peppers

Toast for 30 seconds and promptly transfer into a bowl to cool

Using a coffee grinder or a mortar and pestle, grind finely into a powder form

Add turmeric powder and combine well with all of the ground spices

Store in a tight jar

Eze Rockliff and the Yoruba Singers

On Christmas mornings in Guyana, aromas of Garlic Pork, Pepperpot, coffee, and freshly baked breads complete the morning breakfast traditions in many homes. On Christmas Eve night, homes smell of rum drenched Black Cakes as Christmas carols play in the background from a transistor radio. I want those days back, if even for a moment. I loved the Jingle Bells version of Booker T. I was always awakened by that song on Christmas morning, I remember running into to the kitchen in my new duster or nightie, hurrying to eat my delicious breakfast, then off to open my Christmas present. Finally pounding open walnuts with a hammer, because no one used a nutcracker, or even had one. Firing off caps in the yard with my siblings, the smell still lingering in my memory, Cook-up Rice being prepared as aromas of Stuffed Roast Chicken fills the air... I am entrenched with those memories of my childhood Christmases in Guyana.

Garlic Pork/Lamb/Beef/Chicken

3 lbs of pork, or choice of meat (1 inch thick, & tender cuts preferred)
12 large cloves garlic
2 tbsp of Dried Thyme
1 ½ tbsp sea salt
2 cups of white distilled vinegar
3-4 whole cloves
12-16 sprigs of fresh thyme
½ Cup of fresh thyme leaves (stems reserved) OR
8-10 wiri wiri peppers
½ tsp black pepper
2 cups of boiled water (brought to room temp.)
3 additional cloves of garlic un-peeled

Method:

Wipe meat clean with a damp cloth/paper towel

Using a sharp knife, make little gashes into the meat on both sides

Grind garlic, thyme, and wiri peppers in a food processor/mortar and pestle

Pour this seasoning rub in a small bowl

Using a butter knife or fingers, spread a generous amount to fill the small gashes in meat

Salt and pepper both sides, reserving ½ teaspn salt

Use any left over seasoning mixture to rub on meat slices

Using a wide mouthed glass jar, start by layering pieces of seasoned meat, stacking until all meat has been placed in the jar

Combine vinegar and water and pour gently into the jar of layered meat until it is covered by two inches.

Gently shake the jar gently to distribute evenly, and place thyme stems and cloves in the jar.

Add three cloves of smashed un-peeled garlic as part of the garnish and the peppercorns

Place additional sprigs of thyme on top of jar or slide it down the sides

Sprinkle with ½ teaspoon salt and seal jar tightly

Store in a cool dark place (not refrigerator) and let it rest for 3-5 days

After curing period, drain meat on a rack and discard liquid

Do not allow seasoning in the gashes to fall out In a skillet, pour three tablespoons canola oil

Pan fry on medium heat until nicely browned for about 2-3 minutes per side

Remove and serve with a crusty bread and cold beer or desired beverage

Garlic Meats

** A Portugese contribution, this fantastic treat and almost everyone in Guyana, knows this is a Christmas holiday tradition. Garlic Pork can be served as an appetizer, or between two slices of bread with splash of hot sauce.
Venison also makes a great garlic meat preserve.

My Grandmother Violet made many bottles of Ginger Beer and Mauby at Christmas time. It was and still is a Guyanese tradition. Like typical children, we took for granted the wonderful homemade organic foods and beverages that were readily available to us. Today I long to relive those wonderful memories, and as of late have been creating them in my own kitchen. But unlike the days of having a sunny yard in which the Mauby and Gingerbeer were left to ferment and foam, I opt to place them on my window sill in direct sunlight bringing my beverages to a fruition, even on a winter's day.

Ginger Beer

1 lb of Ginger
10 cups of water
2 cups of dark brown sugar
2 cinnamon sticks
6 cloves
1 4 x 3 inches piece of orange peel

Method:
Grate ginger with the fine side of grater

In a large pot, combine all

ingredients, except cinnamon

Bring to a rapid boil for 10 minutes

Remove from heat and strain

Use a cheese cloth to remove ginger bits

Pour into a large glass jug

Break orange peel and cinnamon sticks in pieces

Add to ginger beer and bring to room temperature

Pour into glass jars and let this rest

Ferment for 5-7 days

Discard cinnamon sticks an orange peel

Serve over crushed ice or cubes

Ginger Beer on the East River of Manhattan

Whenever Grandmother made Pepper Sauce, she made this version because it wasn't so highly concentrated as my Mom's recipe. This meant, that the kids could have a little bit and not burn holes in their tongues. It was kept in direct sunlight in order to protect its vibrant color, and retain its heat. In Guyana, people eat Pepper Sauce as a condiment with every meal.

Guyanese Pepper Sauce

2 lbs of Haberneros peppers
1 cup of distilled white vinegar
1 tbsp of salt
1 tbsp of French's yellow mustard
½ of a large cucumber finely grated (seeds removed)

Method:
Wash peppers and remove stems

In a food processor, or using a mill, grind pepper into a fine consistency

Incorporate the other ingredients well, by stirring with a spoon

If using a food processor, pulse peppers and other ingredients for 30 seconds

Pour mixture into a wide mouth jar that has been sterilized

Place jar by a window where it can get some sunlight for about a week

Remove from window and store in a cool place

This is ready to eat immediately after it is made

Fresh vegetables at a Guyanese Market

guyana's tasty exotic

Granny Da Silva was famous for her beef stew which she served with Bakes or her home made braided bread. This particular stew pairs well with Portuguese Bread, French Baguette or any bread that absorbs its robust gravy. A delicious Red Wine of your choice is a great accompaniment to perfect this meal.

Portuguese Beef Stew

4 lbs of marbled beef chuck
1 lb of veal or beef bones
1 large yellow onion minced finely
2 cups of chopped tomatoes
2 cups of red wine
2 tbsp of fresh thyme minced
½ cup of chopped parsley
½ cup of finely minced celery
2 tbsp of tomato paste
1 tsp of ground allspice
½ tsp clove powder
1 tsp ground cinnamon
1 tsp salt
½ tsp fresh ground black pepper
1 tsp brown sugar
5 cloves of minced garlic
2 tbsp vegetable oil
4 cups of beef stock or water

Method:
With a clean damp cloth wipe meat, then cut into 4 inch pieces

Place meat in a bowl, and add salt, allspice, black pepper

Rinse and drain bones

In deep pot, and on medium heat

Add oil and heat, toss in onion and garlic

Stir and cook for 1 minute, add tomato paste

Cook for about 2 minutes stirring well

Add beef and continue cook until its juices has been absorbed

Add tomatoes and cook for about 3 minutes

Pour red wine and increase heat to high for rapid absorption

Place all other ingredients in pot, and bring to a boil

Reduce to a low simmer and cover

Cook for an hour until a thick gravy is achieved

Garnish with fresh parsley and serve with your favorite bread or rice

Guyanese Cantonese Fried Rice

2 cups of cooked rice
2 lbs of chicken breasts (sliced into 3x3" pieces)
1 medium bunch of bora (long bean)
or 1 cup of french cut fresh string beans (cut in 1" pieces)
1 cup of finely diced carrots
1 cup of thinly sliced cabbage
1 large yellow onion diced
3 tablespoons of soy sauce
1 teaspoon white pepper
1 clove of garlic minced
2 blades of scallion sliced thinly
½ tsp of Chinese five spice powder
4 tbsp vegetable oil
2 tsp cornstarch
1 tbsp grated ginger
2 chicken bouillon(optional)
1 tsp hoisin sauce
1 tsp oyster sauce
1/4 cup of Chinese rice wine
1/3 cup water or chicken stock

Method:
To season chicken, combine cornstarch, ½ tsp

white pepper, ginger, 1 tbsp soy sauce, 1 tsp hoisin sauce, rice wine,

and garlic In a wok or non stick pan using high heat,

saute meat in 1 tbspn oil and

cooked for about 10 minutes, stirring every 2 minutes

Remove meat from pan and set aside

Add onions and ½ tbspn of oil stir fry for

½ minute and remove

Add string beans/bora, and carrots

Stir fry for 3 minutes on high heat

Adding 1/3 cup of water or chicken stock and bouillon

Cook until liquid absorbs about 1 minute

Add cabbage, cook for ½ of a minute and remove

Add 1 tablespoon of oil to wok, and pour rice, soy,

½ teaspoon Chinese five spice powder, ½ teaspoon black pepper, and stir fry and mix well.

Return all other ingredients, and continue to cook

on high heat stirring constantly

Transfer to a serving platter, and garnish with scallions

A definite comfort food, this frugal meal, was mostly prepared on a rainy days. Whenever Grandmother Violet made this tasty and filling rice and peas recipe, it seems we never had enough. The topping contributed to its flavors and fragrance, making it even more desirable. Sharing this recipe is a glimpse into what I ate as a child, and a family treasure that I want to share with you. A great side is a cucumber salad with salt, hot peppers and a twist of lime, add a piece of fried fish and make a fisherman proud. Just promise you will think of me and Granny Violet when you have a brimming bowl of this goodness.

Kedgeree

1 ½ cups of long grain rice
½ cup yellow split peas
1 yellow onion minced
3 large cloves of garlic
½ habernero pepper minced
1 tbsp vegetable oil
2 tbsp ghee
2 tsp salt
2 tsp curry powder
1 tsp parched whole cumin(geera)
4 ½ cups of water

Guyanese Fishermen

Method:
Soak yellow split peas overnight

Drain and set aside

In a heavy bottomed pot add ghee and heat

Add split peas, turmeric, 1 clove of garlic minced,

minced onion, and habernero pepper

Saute for 2-3 minutes on medium heat

Add 1 cup of water and cook until completely reduced

Add rice that has been rinsed, salt, and 3 ½ cups of water

Bring to a rapid boil and reduce to a low simmer

Cook covered tightly for 10 minutes, remove lid stir

Cover and cook for another 10 minutes

Do not worry if Kedgeree seems a little wet, it's part of its charm

In a pan, add oil, 2 cloves of thinly sliced garlic, and parched whole cumin

Cook on medium heat until garlic is medium brown in color

Pour this to the finished Kedgeree and incorporate using a wooden spoon

Serve immediately

Killer Mojito Recipe

3 oz of Good White Rum
2 limes juiced
6 mint leaves
1/4 tsp of Angostura bitters
2 tsp light brown sugar
3 oz of club soda
1 stalk of sugar cane (cut into a 6"strips)
1 sprig of fresh mint for garnish

Method:
Using a muddler or a wooden spoon, bruise mint leaves with sugar in a mug

Add lime juice, and Angostura bitters and stir

Add crushed ice, then pour club soda and white rum

Stir and garnish with sprigs of mint and sugar cane stalk

Salute!

Lai Fun (Chinese Soup)

Pork Balls
Ingredients
½ lb ground pork
1 tbsp corn starch
1 tbsp oyster sauce
1 tsp crushed garlic
1 tbsp rice wine
1 tsp ground ginger
1 tsp sugar
1 tbsp dark soy sauce
1/8 tsp white pepper
½ cup minced water chestnut

Method:
Combine all ingredients well and let rest for 30 minutes
Scoop and form into 10 meat balls
Drop into boiling hot soup and cook for 10 minutes

Soup
Ingredients:
3 cups chicken stock
4 oz of cellophane noodles or rice noodles
1 Lap Cheung (Chinese sausage)
1 tbsp. oyster sauce
8 pork balls
2 bundles of bok choy
½ cup of Chinese mushrooms
1 tbsp chopped scallions
1 tbsp soy sauce
1 tbsp chopped scallions
1 (2") piece of ginger

Method:
Bring stock to a boil and add noodles, mushrooms, ginger, to cook
Saute Lap Cheung for about 2 minutes and set aside
Add pork balls to noodle soup and cook for 10 minutes
Add bok choy and cook for two minutes
Remove and discard the ginger from the soup
Remove from stove and transfer to soup bowls
Add pieces of Lap Cheung to individual bowls
Top with scallions

Mango Sour Condiment

4 cups green mango cubed
1 ½ tsp salt
4 cups of water
4 large wiri wiri peppers

Method:
In a deep pot add green mangoes, salt and peppers

Bring to a rapid boil

Reduce heat to a low medium simmer

Cook for 10 minutes

Cool and use a potato masher to crush in it's liquid

This will thicken and become

Puree and store in a sterilized jar in the refrigerator

** This condiment is generally served with Phoulorie, black pudding, or Dhal Puri**

Mauby at Stabroek Market with a Dhal puri dripping with a mango sour condiment was my special treat for going to the market with my Mom on Saturdays. I loved going to the market anyway, and did not need a treat for my trek. But I could never refuse an ice old Mauby and dhal puri, can any of you?

Mauby Beverage

6 sticks of mauby bark
12 cups of water
2 cinnamon sticks
8 whole cloves
2 cups of sugar (more or less to suit your taste)
1 4" piece of dried orange peel
4 1 inch pieces of dried orange peel
1 piece star anise
6 allspice seeds

Method:
Place all dry ingredients in a deep pot

(except the 4 - 1" pieces of orange peel and 4 cloves)

Add water and boil for about 10 minutes

Let it cool and strain

Pour into 4 individual glass bottles

In each bottle add a clove and a piece of orange peel

Cover tightly and place in direct sunlight to set

A froth will appear on top when mauby is ready

Serve chilled or top with ice cubes

There are so many ways to make this meal, and it's heartiness makes this another Guyanese a comfort food. My memories of going to La Penitence market, and buying the root vegetables, and the green plantains referred to as "provisions", are still vivid. The boats would arrive at the wharf with all the produce, unloaded and distributed to the vendors. whose gab still lingers in raw creolese in my head, and makes me smile whenever I remember my old market jaunts with my Mom Vera.

Mettemgee

3 green plantains
1 lb of eddoes (also known as taro root)
15 or callaloo or spinach leaves
½ lb of pickled pigtails
1 large onion chopped minced
½ tsp salt
1 large habernero pepper
1 tbsp of finely chopped thyme
½ tsp of black pepper
Dumplings (Recipe to follow)

1 lb cassava (yuca)
8 okras
½ lb of salted beef
½ lb of dried cod fish (bacchalau)
2 blades of scallion finely chopped
1 bouillion (optional)
1 medium dry coconut grated
1 tsp brown sugar
2 cups of additional water to cover contents of pot

Method:

Cut salted beef and pigtails into 3 inch pieces, place in a pot and cover with water

Bring to a boil, reduce and cook on low heat for 40 minutes

Drain, reserve meat, and set aside

Boil salted fish for 15 minutes, discard water

Soak in warm water for an additional 15 minutes to render excess salt

Squeeze fish to extract liquid, separate in flakes, and set aside

Peel and wash root vegetables and plantains, then cut into 4 inch pieces

Grate coconut and add 2 cups of water, squeeze and strain to extract milk

or use 1 can coconut milk and 1 cup of water

In a large soup pot, place the precooked meats

Add salted fish, onions, thyme, scallion, black pepper, and brown sugar

Followed by plantains and root vegetables.

Add habernero pepper, coconut milk, and 1 cup of water to cover contents

Bring to a rapid boil, reduce heat to medium, cooking uncovered for 15 minutes

Wash and snip off ends of okras and layer on top

Add dumplings, and steam for exactly 8 minutes

Transfer into a serving platter, and serve immediately

Garnish with sprigs of fresh thyme

Mom's Flaming Hot Pepper Sauce

2 lbs of habernero peppers
1 tbsp of fine sea salt
2 tbsp vegetable oil

Method:

Wash peppers and remove stems.

Place in a food processesor and grind until fine, or use a food mill.

Add oil to a deep frying pan and heat, add pepper and salt and fry for 3-5 minutes

Pour into a jar that has been sterilized, and seal tightly

To retain heat index, let this sit in direct sunlight as often as possible

Do not refrigerate

(A Saturday tradition was freshly baked bread. I especially enjoyed my trek over to Humpreys Bakery on Barr Street, which we were compelled to do in order to conserve gas because of high prices and shortages in the late 1970's. The prep work was a lot of fun, and with trial and error I was sometimes lucky or confronted with unrisen dough. Pride of my handiwork was in place, after all I was just a kid. On one occasion when my dough did not rise, I stubbornly braided the bread and ran to the bakery with my brother carrying the other pan. We paid two quarters for baking, then discovered that it was as hard as rock candy, we cleverly switched our breads with that of another when no one was looking. Then we scurried home, giggling all the way with soft loaves of bread. Those were the days of folly, for my brother Colin and I...)

Grandmother's Hot Pepper Sauce

Mom's Guyanese Bread

4 cups of flour
½ lb butter
2 packs yeast
1 ½ cups of warm water
1 teaspoon salt
1 tbspn baking powder
2 tablespoon of brown sugar

Method:

In a mixing bowl, place brown sugar and yeast

Pour warm water and stir gently, cover with a

kitchen towel and keep in a warm place for yeast to rise

In another bowl, sift all dry ingredients and add

butter breaking it into bits and combining well

After yeast has risen, pour into the flour mixture

If needed add a little water to the yeast mixture

to absorb all the dry ingredients

Knead for about 15 minutes and mold into a ball

Place into a deep bowl and cover.

Set aside and let the dough rise

When dough has doubled it's size, remove and place

on a floured board, cut into fist size pieces and roll out

into bread stick pieces, paste tops together

Braid and baste with olive oil, bake for 30-40 minutes

at 375 degree heated oven

guyana's tasty exotic

Caribbean Roast Beef

My fit for a Goddess Pot Roast

1 beef rump or shoulder roast (approx. 4 lbs)
1 tsp black pepper
1 tbsp soy sauce
1 tbsp black strap molasses
zest of 1 small orange
2 tbsp fresh chopped thyme
6 cloves of minced garlic
2 cups of good red wine (Merlot)
2 tbsp capers drained
1 cup of apricots
6 bay leaves

3 cups of beef stock
1 tsp salt
1 tbsp tomato paste
3 tbsp brown sugar
1/4 cup chopped parsley
2 tbsp anchovy paste
1 cup of fresh cocktail white onions
1 cup of imported black olives pitted
1 cup pitted prunes
1 cup of pineapple cubes

Method:

Heat oven to 325 degrees

Clean meat by wiping with a damp cloth

Combine salt, pepper, anchovies, molasses, soy sauce, brown sugar

thyme, and garlic to make a marinade using a mortar and pestle or food processor

Use a sharp knife to pierce meat

Pour marinade on meat, and lather pushing some into meat opening

Let this sit in the refrigerator overnight

Before cooking, this must rest in room temperature for at least 35 minutes

Add oil to heavy bottomed pot or Dutch oven on high heat

Add meat and its marinade and sear to seal in juices

Pour wine over roast and continue to cook on high until reduced in half

Add all other ingredients

Cover and bring to a boil

Transfer to oven, and roast for 2 ½ - 3 hrs

During roasting, baste with liquid every 30 minutes

Remove and discard bay leaves

Let this rest on a cutting board for 30 minutes

Slice meat in thick pieces

Lay on a deep platter and spoon juices with fruit pieces on top

Serve with buttered egg noodles

Garnish with sprigs of parsley

Okra can be quite delicious when prepared correctly. The method to the okra madness is to "avoid the slimy", as described in my home back in the day. "Avoiding the slimy", can be done by first washing your okras, wiping them dry, then air drying for about 30 minutes. The next step is snipping of the ends, and slicing into 1/4 inch thick rounds. More importantly is to have a very hot pan for cooking. While there are many ways to prepare okra, this is one of the most popular ways to prepare it.

Pan Fried Okra with Shrimp

1 lb okra
1 lb shrimp
1 tsp salt
½ tsp black pepper
4 tbsp vegetable oil
1 medium onion
3 cloves of garlic
1 tsp hot red pepper (optional)
3 springs of thyme chopped
OR
1 tbsp dried thyme crumbled

Method:
Wash, towel dry and air dry okra for 30 minutes

Slice into ½ inch rounds

Chop onion, garlic, and thyme

In a wok or non stick skillet, pour 1 tbsp of oil

Add shrimp, stir and cook for 1 minute

Remove shrimp and set aside

Pour remainder of oil to pan

Add onion, stir fry for 1 minute

Add garlic and hot pepper and cook for 30 seconds.

Add okra, thyme, salt, and pepper and stir well

Keep heat high until all the slime has dissolved

Turn every 2-3 minutes to cook evenly

After slime is gone, return shrimp to pot and continue cooking

Okra will appear slightly browned when done

Serve immediately over steamed rice.

Orange Ginger Roast Pork Loin

2-3 lb pork loin
1 cup of orange juice concentrate
1/4 cup of honey
2 tbsp brown sugar
1/3 cup soy sauce
1 tbsp fresh ground ginger
2 tbsp chopped scallions
1/3 cup apricot jam
2 tbsp black sesame oil
1 tsp Dijon mustard
½ tsp ground white pepper
½ tsp Chinese five spice powder
1 tbsp fresh ground garlic

Method:
Combine all ingredients except the pork to create a marinade

Place pork loin in a plastic bag and drench with marinade

Make sure that pork loin is well covered with marinade

Seal tight and refrigerate overnight

Remove and let sit at room temperature before cooking

Preheat oven to 375 degrees

Place pork in a roasting pan, affixed with a meat thermometer

Roast for 25 minutes, thermometer should register to 160 degrees

Remove and rest for 15 minutes before serving

Paratha Roti

4 cups all purpose flour
1 tsp baking powder
½ tsp salt
1 tbsp sugar
1 tbsp of melted ghee (clarified butter) or oil
2 cups of tepid water (more or less of)
1 cup of vegetable oil

Method:
Sift all dry ingredients together and mix

Drizzle ghee and continue to mix

Slowly dispense water, binding into a dough

Moisten dough with a little water or oil to retain softness

Cover with a warm kitchen towel or saran wrap

Allow dough to rest for 30-45 minutes at room temperature

Cut dough into 8 equal pieces or about the size of a baseball

On a lightly floured board, roll out into 6-8 inch rounds

Drizzle 1 tsp vegetable oil on top of dough and spread evenly

Cut a slit from the top center right down to the middle

Start from one end and roll dough into a cone shape

Tuck ends to meet in the center on both sides and set aside

Cover and let this rest for 30 minutes

Place a non stick flat pan on medium heat

Using a spoon, drizzle a half of tsp of ghee onto the pan

Flatten and mold a piece of oiled dough into a flat disk

On a floured board, roll into a round shape about 8"in diameter

Place on the hot pan, turn after 5 seconds or when you see little welts forming

Use a pastry brush to distribute oil evenly on roti

Flip roti after 10 seconds

Apply oil to the other side and flip

Continue to cook it for 10-12 seconds or until it puffs up or gets cooked

Cooking time generally takes 40-50 seconds to fully cook a roti

Using a spatula, remove cooked roti and place in kitchen towel

Using both hands, clap and release to remove air and soften

Repeat 3-4 times

Fold cooked roti into half and place on a serving platter

Cover loosely with a kitchen towel

Clapping removes air from the roti, making it soft and flaky

Serve this with pan fried vegetables, stews or curries or the way most Guyanese folks like it - buttered

Pastry Dough

3 cups of flour
1 ½ sticks or 12 tbspns of cold butter
1/4 cup of shortening or vegetable oil
1 teaspoon salt
8 tbspns of iced water

Method:
Sift flour and salt in a large mixing bowl
Dice butter into tiny cubes and add
Add shortening or vegetable oil
Use fingertips to mix together
Add cold water one tbspn at a time or until all dry ingredients has been absorbed
Mold into a ball, wrap in plastic
Refrigerate for 30 minutes before using

* tthis can be used for all recipes requiring pastry dough

Pepperpot

1 lb of marbled chuck steak (large cubes)
1 lb of short ribs
1 lb of oxtail
1 cow's feet (cut up in 2" pieces)
3 cups of cassareep
2 large habernero peppers(place whole in the pot)
2 (2") pieces of dried orange peel
2 (3") pieces of cinnamon sticks
6 cloves
6 cloves of garlic
1 tbsp coarse salt
1/4 cup of fresh thyme minced
1 ½ tsp black pepper
2 small or 1 large bouillon
enough water to cover meat about 6" above

Method:
Wash and place all ingredients in a large soup pot

Bring to a rapid boil and reduce to a medium to low simmer

Cook for 1 hour covered with a tight lid

Add 1-2 cups of hot water upon discretion to cover meat if needed

Remove whole steam peppers, and crush with a fork

Return crushed peppers to pot

Continue to cook for another hour on low simmer

Remove and discard orange peel

Do not serve, since this needs a lot of rest time to macerate

Transfer to a bowl and refrigerate overnight

Fat will rise to the top and become hardened

Carefully lift off and discard

Return to pot, do not be deterred by the gelatinous appearance

Heat on a low simmer covered, the sauce will start to return

Taste and adjust seasonings accordingly if needed

Heat on low, until the entire stew is bubbling and appears piping hot

Ladle a generous amount, and serve with fresh home made Guyanese bread

Reheat on stove daily, before serving.

** The longer Pepperpot is nurtured by daily stove-top reheating, the more intensified the flavors become **.

Phulourie

1 cup split peas (soaked overnight)
6 cloves of minced garlic
1 onion grounded 1 tsp turmeric
2 tsp geera 1 tsp baking powder 1 cup flour 2 tsp salt 1 tbsp hot pepper sauce
1/4 cup chopped cilantro (optional) 3/4 cup water 1 quart oil for frying

Method:
Blend or grind soaked split peas with 1 cup of water

Blend or grind onion, pepper sauce, garlic, and cilantro

Transfer ground peas and ground seasonings into a large bowl

Add turmeric, geera, salt, flour, and baking powder and mix well

Heat oil in a deep frying pan to 400 degree temp.

(use a thermometer for accuracy) and reduce heat to medium

Drop about 1 tbsp of batter by hand in formation of a small ball

Turn after brown about ½ minute and repeat the same cooking time on the other side

Remove and drain on an absorbent paper towel

Serve with Mango Sour condiment (see index for recipe)

Ham, Cheese & Herb Scones

3 cups all purpose flour
2 tbsp sugar
1 tbsp baking powder
½ tsp fine salt
3/4 cup butter cold
1 cup buttermilk
1 egg beaten
½ cup diced ham
½ cup grated sharp cheddar cheese
3 tbsp fresh herbs (scallion, thyme, hot pepper, minced)

Method:
Preheat the oven to 425 degrees.

Line one baking sheet with parchment paper

In a large mixing bowl combine the flour, sugar, baking powder and salt.

Use a pastry cutter to combine and form a coarse crumbly dough.

Stir in the buttermilk, ham, cheese, and fresh herbs

Form a dough, turn onto a floured surface

Roll out carefully into a 2 inch thick round

Cut into 8 triangles

Place onto the baking sheet

Brush with beaten egg

Bake for 20 minutes or until golden in color

Tip:

If you don't have buttermilk available make it by

Adding 2 tbsp of lemon juice or white vinegar to 1 cup of whole milk

Let this rest for 10 minutes

It's fall here in New York, which means it's pie season. So let the baking begin. I bake pies all year round, in the summer it's Peach Cobbler, Apple Tart Tartin, Mixed Berry Pie, German Plum Cake, Apricot, Cherry, Plum Pie, and of course my favorite... Banana Cream Pie. So a few months ago I designed a pie for my friends who would appreciate a pie with a Caribbean twist. If you want something new and amazing, try making this Pineapple Galette.

Pineapple Galette with Cherry Jelly Glaze

1 fresh pineapple peeled, cored and sliced into rounds
½ cup of brown sugar
1 tbsp of ground cinnamon
1 tablespoon of powdered ginger
½ tsp salt
1 tbsp corn starch
½ cup of pineapplle juice
4 6 tbsp cherry glaze (German Sour Cherry works best)
1 cinnamon stick for garnish
Pie Crust (recipe in index)

Method:
Heat Oven to 375 degrees

Grease a 9" pie dish, a glass Pyrex Pie Dish works well In a bowl,

combine sugar, cinnamon, ginger, salt, and corn starch

Coat pineapple slices with mixture using every bit

Allow this to macerate for 10 minutes

Roll out pie dough to 13" round, and place in baking dish

Starting from the center, place pineapple slices overlapping each other

Use all slices even if you have to pile the rings on top of each other

Drizzle pineapple juice in crevices and openings between the slices

Fold edges of dough to cover most of the pie

Place cinnamon stick in the peek a boo center

Sprinkle with cinnamon sugar

Bake for 1 hour until golden and bubbling

Brush generously with cherry jelly glaze or any fruit jelly of your preference

Continue to bake for another 25 minutes

Remove from oven and rest for 30 minutes before slicing into wedgesSweet Pastry Dough

Sweet Pastry Dough

3 cups of flour
1 ½ or 12 tbsp sticks of butter (cold and salted)
1/4 cup of shortening
2 egg yolks
1 ½ cups of sugar
1 teaspoon salt
6 tbspns of cold milk

Method:
Sift all dry ingredients

Dice and incorporate butter and shortening

Beat egg yolks with milk

Incorporate with dry ingredients

Mold into a ball, wrap in plastic

Refrigerate for 30 minutes before using

This is my son Martin's absolute favorite meal on a cold winter's day. This can be made a couple of days ahead and reheated in the oven before serving.

Martin's Favorite Potted Chicken

1 (4-5 lb) chicken quartered
2 parsnips peeled and cut in 3" pieces
4 large carrots peeled and cut into 3" pieces
½ cup of finely chopped parsley
1 cup of dry white wine
1 tspn salt
1 tbsp of sweet paprika
2 tablespoon of olive oil
1 jar of Dijon mustard as a condiment (optional)

1 large onion peeled and quartered
3 bay leaves
1 lb of new potatoes washed and cut into halves
1 large celery rib cut into 3" pieces
2 cups of chicken stock
½ tspn white pepper
4-5 cloves of garlic finely minced
4 sprigs of fresh thyme

Method:

Preheat oven to 350 degrees

Season chicken with salt, pepper and paprika

Place Dutch oven or a heavy bottomed pot on high heat

Pour olive oil, and brown chicken for about three minutes on both sides

Remove chicken and place on a platter

Add carrots, potatoes, celery, parsnips, onions, and garlic to pot

Saute for 3-4 minutes

Return chicken and arrange it on top of vegetables

Add all other ingredients, cover and transfer to oven

Place on middle rack for even cooking for 90 minutes

Promptly remove from oven and place on a cooling rack

Let this rest for 25 minutes

Transfer chicken to a platter, and arrange vegetables around chicken

Discard bay leaves, and drizzle sauce on top

Garnish with sprigs of fresh parsley

Serves four, and harmonizes quite well with a side of Dijon mustard,

Horseradish, or your condiment of choice

** Can be made a day ahead, reheats well **

Martin's Favorite Potted Chicken

The British came and left this one for us. We added more flavor, and called it Guyanese. That is just how we operate when it comes to food, and after you've had our version, you will understand why this Pub Style Beef and Stout Pie is a Guyanese specialty.

Pub style Beef and Stout Pie

4 lbs chuck steak cubed
1 lb small white mushrooms quartered
2 cups of beef broth
3 tbsp tomato paste
1 tbsp ground coriander
1 cup of carrots diced
4 tbsp fresh chopped parsley
1 tsp ground black pepper
1 cup all purpose flour

1 cups of white pearl onions peeled
3 cups of good Irish stout
3 tbsp fresh chopped thyme
6 cloves of garlic minced
1 lb potatoes diced (skin on)
10 tbsp olive oil
1 tsp Kosher salt
½ lb of Stilton cheese crumbled

Method:
Heat oven to 325 degrees

In a Dutch oven (or a heavy bottomed pot) heat 2 tbsp of oil

Add mushrooms, onions, carrots, and potatoes and saute until brown

Remove and set aside

Season beef with salt, pepper, and ground coriander and coat with flour

Add 3 tbsp of oil in the same pot and heat

Add half of the steak and cook to sear and remove

Repeat with the other half, remove and set aside

Add ½ cup of stout to pot to de-glaze, and scrape brown bits

Pour this onto sauteed vegetables

Return pot to stove and heat remainder of olive oil

Add garlic and thyme and cook for one minute

Stir in tomato paste and cook for one minute

Return meat to pot and coat well, cooking for one minute

Return vegetables, add stout, and beef stock to pot

Cover and bring to a rapid boil

Transfer to oven and cook for 2 ½ hours for ambient cooking

Remove and add prepared pastry crust

Top with Stilton cheese crust and bake in a 425 degree oven for an additional 35 minutes

Stilton Cheese Crust:
Add ½ lb of crumbled Stilton cheese to pie crust dough recipe before mixing

Roll out, cover Dutch oven with dough, and brush with beaten egg n

Return to oven baking for 35 minutes, rest for 15 minutes before serving

Pulao

2 cups basmati rice or any long grain rice

12 green beans or 4 long bean (bora) cut into 1" pieces

1 medium carrot or squash diced

½ cup frozen green peas (optional)

8-10 florets cauliflower(optional)

2 medium onions sliced thinly

3 tbsp ghee

1 tsp toasted cumin seeds

1 cinnamon stick

3-4 green cardamoms

3-4 cloves

1 tbsp black peppercorns

2 bay leaves

1 tsp salt

3 chopped green chillies or hot pepper of your choice

2 tbsp of finely minces cilantro for garnishing(optional)

Method:
Soak rice for a half an hour in cold water

In a saute pan add ghee on a medium heat

Add onions and fry until browned and slightly crisped

Add cumin cinnamon, cardamom, cloves,

peppercorns, and bay leaves

Saute for 1 minute

Add onion and saute for 2 minutes

Add vegetables and saute for 1 minute

Drain and add rice

Stir fry for a minute

Stir in 4 cups of water and salt, bring to a rapid boil

Reduce to medium heat and continue to cook for 5 minutes

Stir occasionally and cook until most of the liquid has been absorbed

Add vegetables, reduce heat

Cook uncovered for 6-8 minutes or until rice is cooked

Remove from stove, and let it set covered for 5 minutes

Garnish with chopped chillies and cilantro before serving

** For added protein, add a cup of cooked chick peas**

Guyana's pumpkin is so flavorful,. It's texture is meaty and taste distinct.

One can enjoy it many ways, I love a good pumpkin stir fried with shrimp and herbs served with roti, or else a delicious pumpkin conkie. Then of course there is always pumpkin fritters.

But this pumpkin pie is to die for, especially when served with a large scoop of ice-cream.

Pumpkin Pie

1/4 cup all purpose flour

1 cup of steamed pumpkin mashed

1/4 cup of milk or heavy cream

1/3 cup of brown sugar

1 tsp cinnamon grounded

1/4 tsp ground cloves

1 tsp of grated ginger

1/4 tsp grated nutmeg

1/4 tsp salt

2 eggs beaten

½ can of condensed milk

½ tsp of ground cardamom

1 9x12" round sweet pastry dough (see index for recipe)

Method:
Preheat oven to 375 degrees

Grease a round pie dish (9x12)

Roll our pastry dough, and place it in the pie dish

Fold and press sides to form a decorative crust

In a mixing bowl, combine all ingredients well

Pour mixture into the pie dish

Dot with little pieces of butter

Bake for 40 minutes

Let this rest for 15 minutes before serving

Pairs well with a scoop of ice-cream or whipped cream

See index for sweet pasty dough recipe.

Roasted Red Snapper

1 (3) lb red snapper gutted, and de-scaled
3 tbsp fresh thyme
4 cloves of garlic
3 wiri wiri peppers or chillies
1 large yellow onion
3 medium tomatoes
3 blades of scallion (green onion)
5 leaves of African thyme(Broad leaf thyme) optional
2 limes
1 lemon
1 tsp grounded mustard seeds
2 tbsp sesame seeds
½ tsp ground black pepper
4 tbsp butter
1 tsp sea salt

Method:
Heat oven to 500 degrees

Rinse red snapper, and squeeze lemon juice inside and out

Rinse and pat dry to remove excess water

Cut slits into fish and set aside

Grind garlic, thyme, African thyme, scallions, and wiri wiri peppers

Place this mixture, into the slits of fish

Use the remainder to lather the inside of the fish

Sprinkle salt, pepper, sesame seeds, and mustard seed on both side of the fish

Place some slices of butter on the bottom of a flat roasting pan

Place snapper on top of butter

Top with slices of onions, tomatoes, and slices of butter

Squeeze lime juice generously over fish

Roast for 30 minutes uncovered

Broil for 2 minutes

Rest for 10 minutes before serving

Serve with rice pilaf or crusty bread

Traditional Indo Caribbean Dancers

Roath

A favorite with many, this sweet is generally made for Hindu religious functions.

6 cups of flour
3 tbsp ghee (clarified butter)
½ cup raisins chopped
½ cup cherries diced
1 cup of milk
1 cup of white sugar
2 tbsp black poppy seeds (optional)
1 tsp ground cardamom
1/4 tsp fine salt

Additional ghee for frying

Method:
Combine all 9 ingredients together

Knead into a firm dough and form into the size of a tennis ball

Roll into 2 inch thick disks about 4 inches in circumference

In a frying pan, melt 4 tbsp ghee on low to medium heat

Fry until golden brown for about 3 -5 minutes on each side

Check for doneness by breaking open

Interior should appear flaky

Sprinkle with powdered sugar

Roath with Chocolates

Salara

3 cups flour
1 whole egg and 1 egg yolk beaten
3 tbsp butter
½ cup sugar
1 tsp salt
1 cup milk
1 pack of yeast (1/4 oz)
1 egg + 1 tbsp milk (egg wash)

Filling:
1 ½ cups of grated coconut
½ cup sugar
1 tsp cinnamon
1 tbsp vanilla extract
2 tbsp red food coloring

Combine all the filling ingredients in a large bowl and set aside

Method:
Warm milk on the stove top and set aside

In a bowl sift flour, sugar, and salt

Add yeast and incorporate well

Mix beaten egg and warm milk

Mix into dry ingredients to form a soft dough

Cover, and let rest until double in size for about 1 hour

Knead and divide it in half

Roll out into a rectangular shape

Brush it with melted butter

Spread half of the filling on to dough evenly

Roll into thirds

Pinch and seal edges together with water

Cover and let rest for an hour

Brush with egg wash

Pre heat oven 375 degrees

Bake for 30 minutes or until golden brown

Rest for 20 minutes and cut into 3" slices

Salt Cod with Potatoes and Eggs

1 lb salt cod
1 lb potatoes
½ cup olive oil
3 cloves of garlic
1 yellow onion sliced thinly
1 tsp ground black pepper
1/4 cup of black olives chopped
1 cup chopped tomatoes
6 eggs beaten
2 tbsp freshly chopped parsley
2 tbsp chopped scallion
½ habanero pepper minced

Method:

Soak cod in cold water overnight

Remove skin and bones, and flake into pieces

Peel and slice potatoes into 1" thick rounds

Heat olive oil in a non stick pan and add potatoes

Brown on both sides

Drain, remove, and set aside

Add onions and garlic to skillet and cook for two minutes

Add tomatoes and cook for 4 minutes

Toss in habanero, parsley, scallions, and eggs

Return potatoes and cook on low heat

Crumble cod pieces over skillet and stir

Toss in olives

Serve with rustic Portuguese bread

Salt Fish Cakes

1 lb of dried salted fish
3 tbsp of plain breadcrumbs
1 egg lightly beaten
½ cup of finely minced cilantro
1 medium finely diced onion
½ tsp of ground black pepper
1 tbsp of baking powder
½ cup of all purpose flour
1 finely diced scotch bonnet pepper(optional)
½ cup of milk
1 tsp of cornstarch
Oil for deep frying

Method:

Heat oil to 375 temperature using a thermometer for accuracy

Reconstitute salted fish by boiling for about 20 minutes

Drain, remove skin and bones

Using a fork flake fish

Add all ingredients and mix well

Scoop a tablespoon and drop into hot oil

Fry for 1 minute each on both sides, or until brown

Serve on top of a bed of lettuce, cucumber, and tomatoes.

My primitive foot grater demo

Shepherds Pie

For Filling:
2 lbs ground lamb
1 large yellow onion diced finely
6 carrots cut into 3 inch pieces
1 tbsp of freshly chopped parsley
1 tbsp of freshly chopped tarragon (optional)
½ tbsp of freshly chopped rosemary (optional)
1 tsp of freshly chopped thyme
1 tsp of grated nutmeg
1 tbsp of ground coriander
½ tsp black pepper
1 ½ tsp of salt
2 tbsp of canola oil
1 tbsp of Worcestershire sauce
2 tbsp of tomato paste
1 cup of beef or lamb stock

For Topping
4 cups of mashed potatoes
1 teaspoon of French's yellow mustard
4 tablespoons of melted butter
½ cup of sour cream
1 cup of grated or shredded cheddar cheese
½ tsp white pepper

Mix all topping ingredients together, except for cheddar cheese and set aside

Method:
In a skillet, brown onion in canola oil
Add meat and saute for three minutes
Add remaining filling ingredients, except for stock
Saute for 2 minutes more
Add stock
Bring to a rapid boil and reduce to a low simmer until sauce is thickened and not runny
Pour into a casserole dish
To prepare topping, combine all the topping ingredients, except for cheddar cheese
Spoon potatoes onto the meat mixture
Spread evenly with a damp spatula
Sprinkle shredded cheddar cheese generously covering the top
Cover and bake for 30 minutes in a 400 degree oven
Bake uncovered for 10 minutes more or until golden brown
Garnish with fresh chives or parsley

Shrimp Exotic

1 lb of cold prawns or extra large shrimp
3 tbsp fresh lime juice
1 large tomato chopped coarsely
1 Vidalia onion sliced and chopped coarsely
1/4 cup fresh chopped cilantro
1 tsp hot pepper sauce
1 cup of sweet ripe mango diced
1 cup of sweet pineapple diced
½ tsp salt
3 tbsp walnut oil or light olive oil
½ tsp fresh ground black pepper
2 tbsp ketchup
2 medium sized ripe avocado diced
Boston or Bibb lettuce leaves

Method:
In a small bowl, combine lime juice, hot pepper sauce,

ketchup, oil, salt, and black pepper

In a large bowl, combine shrimp, chopped tomatoes, onions,

mangoes, pineapple, and cilantro

Drizzle dressing and toss well

Return to refrigerator and chill for 2 hours

Toss in avocado

Assemble by scooping large spoonfuls and filling into lettuce leaves

Serve immediately

Fresh Shrimp

It isn't Easter in Guyana with out Shrove Pancakes, picnic baskets, and kite flying on the seawalls in Georgetown.

Tuesday Shrove Pancakes

For Pancakes
2 1/4 cups flour
2 tbsp sugar
1/4 tsp cinnamon
1 tsp dry yeast
½ tsp salt
1 tbsp vanilla extract
1 tbsp rose water
3 eggs
1 1/4 cup of warm milk

Method:
Mix flour, sugar, cinnamon, salt, and yeast to a large bowl

Beat eggs, rose water, vanilla, a milk in another bowl

Add this carefully to the flour mixture

Make sure to keep this batter very moist but not runny

Place in a warm place to rise covered with clean cloth

Let this rest for 40 minutes or until it has risen and appears light and airy

During this resting period, make syrup (recipe below) and set aside

Place a deep frying pan on high heat and add oil for deep frying

Using a thermometer, place to check the temp which should be 350 degrees

Scoop with hand, form into a balls, and drop into the hot oil

Be sure to flip to the other side to ensue golden color on both sides

This cooks quickly, so reduce heat to low

Remove with a slotted spoon and drain on an absorbent towel or paper towel

After you're done frying all, add them to the bowl of syrup

For Syrup
2 cups water
1 ½ cups caster sugar (same as fine white sugar)
1 small cinnamon stick
2 cloves
1 star anise
2 green cardamom pods

Place water, sugar, star anise, cinnamon stick, cloves, and cardamom in a deep pot

Bring to a boil until thick and syrupy in consistency, but not gooey

Remove promptly, and pour into a large bowl

Fry pancakes, drop into syrup, and mix

Ladle into dessert bowls

Garnish with sprigs of fresh mint

Siew Yuk (Cantonese Crispy Roast Pork)

3 lbs pork shoulder (skin on)
1 tsp fine salt
1 tsp coarse salt
1 ½ tsp white pepper
1 ½ tsp five spice powder
2 tsp of ginger powder
1 tsp garlic powder
1 tsp of msg (optional)

Method:
Combine salt, white pepper, five spice powder, garlic powder, and ginger to form a dry rub
Wipe meat and stab small slits into skin
Apply generously to meat, inserting into skin
Seal with plastic wrap and refrigerate for 3 days
Turn position of meat daily
Heat oven to 500 degrees
Remove from refrigerator, uncover, and bring to room temp.
Place meat skin side up on a wire rack and sprinkle with coarse salt
Place in oven and roast for 20 minutes
Reduce oven temp. to 300 degrees and roast for
Roast for 1 hour
Remove and rest for 15 minutes
Best carved, using an electric knife for precision and easy cutting
Serve with steamed Jasmine rice and chopped scallions

Sizzling Ginger Chicken

1 whole chicken cut into quarters
1 head garlic
2 tbsp brown sugar
1 cup soy sauce
1 tbsp sliced ginger
1 cup of sesame oil
1 cup of Chinese rice wine
1 tsp white pepper
1/4 cup of fresh whole basil leaves

Method:
Make a marinade of sesame oil, soy sauce, rice wine, brown sugar, and white pepper

Pour this onto the chicken and marinate over night

Before cooking, let meat come to room temperature to remove the chill

Heat Dutch oven or heavy bottomed pot on high heat

Add chicken pieces without marinade and garlic, ginger, and basil

Separate garlic cloves and add to pot

Turn chicken to sear both sides

Continue to cook pouring marinade

Scrape bits from the bottom

Stir and simmer on a low flame

After liquid has been absorbed, chicken will appear glazed.

Serve immediately

Sorrel is very popular in the Caribbean and has now made its way into the culinary arenas of many restaurants and kitchens here in the States. Infused into seafood and meat dishes, sorrel enhances by giving color and intensifies flavors with a unique twist.

Sorrel Beverage

2 cups of fresh Sorrel
Or 1 ½ cups of dried
12 cups of water
3 tablespns of brown sugar
1 3-inch piece of orange peel
1 3-inch piece of cinnamon stick
2-3 cloves
½ cup of sugar

Method:
Using a large pitcher, place sorrel, 3 tablespoons sugar, orange peel, cinnamon stick, and cloves

Bring water to a rapid boil and pour directly into pitcher

Stir and cover

Let this sit at room temperature for 24 hours

Strain and sweeten with sugar

Fill in bottles or jars and refrigerate

Serve chilled or with crushed ice

Sorrel Beverage

Spicy Sweet Wing Dings

3 lbs chicken wings(cut in half)
½ cup of honey
1 tbsp Garam Masala
1 tsp ground black pepper
1 tsp cayenne pepper
1 tsp salt
1 tsp fresh ground ginger
2 tbsp molasses
1 tbsp vegetable oil
6 cloves of garlic minced finely
1 tbsp sherry vinegar
2 blades of finely chopped scallion

Method:
Combine honey, garam masala, black pepper, cayenne pepper, salt,

ginger, molasses, garlic and oil and sherry vinegar, and mix well

pour onto chicken wings and marinate overnight in the refrigerator

Place these wings on a wire rack

Broil for 2 minutes on both sides to seal in juices

Switch oven to bake mode to 400 degrees, and bake for 40 minutes

Transfer to platter, top with chopped scallions and serve

Ham Hock Split Peas Soup

Split Pea Soup

2 lb chuck steak cut into chunks
1 lb beef bones
1 cup split peas
1 lb eddoes (taro root)
2 green plantains
1 lb cassava (yuca)
1 tsp salt
½ tsp black pepper
2 small beef bouillon or 1 large
1 large yellow onion diced
½ cup diced celery
1 tbsp freshly chopped thyme or 1 tsp dried thyme crumbled
6 bay leaves
6 cups water
2 wiri wiri peppers (optional)

Method:
In a large stock pot, add split peas, water, beef, bay leaves, onion, celery, and thyme

Bring to a rapid boil

Reduce to low heat and cook for 45 minutes

Add all other ingredients, and additional water to cover up to 3 inches

Cover pot and cook for 30 minutes or until vegetables are fork tender

To determine completion broth should be smooth and thick in consistency

Ladle into soup bowls and top with chopped scallions

Split Peas Cook-up

2 cups of Carolina long grain rice
½ cup of yellow split peas
5-6 springs of fresh thyme chopped
2-3 wiri wiri peppers minced (optional)
1 medium onion chopped
1 cup of coconut milk
3 cups of water
1 lb of salted pigtails (optional)
1 lb beef chuck steak cut into small cubes
2 cloves of garlic minced
½ tsp black pepper
2 blades of scallion chopped finely
1 tbsp vegetable oil

Method:
In a sauce pot, submerge pigtails in cold water covering well and bring to a rapid boil
Reduce to a simmer, and cook until pigtails are fork tender for about 1 ½ hour
Discard water and reserve meat
In another pot, add oil and heat
Saute onion, garlic and pepper for about 2-3 minutes
Add beef, pigtails, and split peas and stir for 2-3 minutes
Add water to cover and thyme and bring to a rapid boil, reducing to a simmer
Cook for 40 minutes
Add rice, coconut milk, black pepper
Add 1 ½ cups of water and bring to boiling point, reduce to a very low simmer for about 20 minutes. Stir once and simmer on low for about 20 minutes
After rice is cooked, about 20 minutes, sprinkle top with green onion. Serve hot

Split Peas Creole Soup

2 green plantains (peeled and cut into 3" pieces)
1 lb eddoes (taro root) (peeled and cut into 3" pieces)
1 lb cassava (yucca) (peeled and cut into 3"pieces)
2 lbs of chuck beef (washed and cut into 3" pieces)
1 cup of yellow split peas rinsed
2 bay leaves
1 tbsp salt
1 tsp black pepper
2 tbsp leaf thyme minced
2 beef bouillon
1 large onion minced
4 tbsp chopped celery
2 tbsp chopped African thyme (optional)
2-3 wiri wiri peppers whole
1 cup of cubed pumpkin
2 ears of corn (cut each piece into 3" pieces)
3 blades of chopped scallion
Water to cook

Method:
In a large soup pot, add split peas, beef and bones, bay leaf, celery, onions,
African thyme, fine leaf thyme, salt, pepper, bouillon, and wiri wiri peppers
Add enough water to cover up to 4" over the ingredients
Bring to a rapid boil, and reduce to a low simmer
Cook for 45 minutes or until meat is fork tender and split peas have somewhat melted
Add corn, plantains, cassava, eddoes, and enough water to cover vegetables
Cover and cook for 15 minutes on medium heat
Add pumpkin and cook for another 10 minutes
Ladle into soup bowls
Top with scallion and serve immediately

** Dumplings are a great addition to this soup, see index for the recipe, and cooking suggestions on how to cook them in a soup**

Savory Stuffed Cabbage

1 lb ground chuck steak
1/4 lb bacon cooked to crispiness and chopped (optional)
3 tbsp parsley finely chopped
1/4 cup finely minced shallots
4 cloves garlic minced
1 slice white bread soaked in water (crust discarded)
½ cup of long grain uncooked rice
2 eggs beaten with a ½ cup of water (egg mixture)
½ tsp ground nutmeg
1 tbsp ground coriander
1 large green cabbage
6-8 large carrots peeled, sliced,
and seasoned with salt and pepper
1 onion minced finely
1 ½ cup of vegetable, chicken or beef stock
1 tbsp fresh thyme chopped
1 tsp salt + 1 tsp extra salt to steaming cabbage
1 tsp ground black pepper
1 tbsp Worcestershire sauce
1 tsp yellow mustard

Method:
In a mixing bowl, add ground chuck, bacon, parsley, shallots, soaked white bread, rice, coriander, pepper, 1 tsp salt, Worcestershire sauce, nutmeg, thyme, black pepper, garlic, onion, mustard, and egg mixture

Combine well, and refrigerate for 1 hour

Place a large pot of water to boil

Upon boiling point add 1 tsp salt

Carefully add cabbage simmer on medium heat for 5 minutes

Remove and cut off leaves, returning cabbage to the pot to further cook inner leaves

Remove semi cooked leaves, and continue process until you have about 12- 14 leaves

Set aside

Divide the meat equally to appropriate for the amount of cabbage leaves

Lay cabbage leaves on a board, place meat mixture in the center

Roll once, then fold top and bottom toward center

Continue to roll and stick a toothpick to hold together

Season carrots with salt and pepper, and place in a Pyrex

Pour stock in a Pyrex and place cabbage rolls with ends facing bottom of pyrex

Cover loosely with aluminum foil or a Pyrex cover

Bake in a 350@ oven for 45 minutes

Serve with mashed potatoes, or buttered egg noodles

Stuffed Eggplants

2 medium sized eggplants
½ lb ground beef or turkey
2 cloves garlic minced
1 tbsp tomato paste
1 tbsp tomato puree
1 tbsp thyme chopped finely
1 tbsp parsley finely minced
½ tsp sea salt
1 tbsp olive oil
1/4 cup of green olives coarsely chopped
1 tsp Worcestershire Sauce
½ tsp ground black pepper
½ cup plain bread crumbs
1/4 cup of Parmesan cheese
1/4 cup of water or meat stock

Method:
Heat oven to 375 degrees

Cut the eggplants in half lengthwise

Brush with olive oil

Place face down on a flat baking sheet

Bake for about 20 minutes

Cool and scoop out pulp to separate from skin

Keep skin in tact

Mince pulp, set aside, and cool in a bowl

Add all other ingredients, and mix roughly

Fill the eggplant shells with the stuffing

Top with Parmesan cheese

Place in the oven and bake for another 25 minutes

Serve with slices of crusty bread

Sweet Lobster Pomegranate Salad

4 cups of lobster meat
Fresh Lettuce or one of your choice
1 avocado diced
1 cup beets diced
1 head of Bibb lettuce
1 large mango julienne
1 red pepper julienne

Dressing:
1 cup pomegranate juice
1/4 tsp salt
1 tsp soy
½ tsp black pepper
2 limes juiced
1 tsp sugar
1/4 cup light olive oil

Method:
Combine all of the dressing ingredients and set aside

Drizzle dressing on lobster, mango, avocado, beets, and red pepper

Place strategically into pocket of Bibb lettuce

Top with fresh cracked pepper

Steel Pan players during Independence day Celebration

Tropical Sangria with nectars du jour

1 cup of tamarind nectar
1 cup pineapple juice
1 cup orange juice
1 cup of guava nectar
6 oz Dry Spanish red wine
12 oz Sherry
½ cup diced oranges (skin on)
½ cup diced mangoes (skin on)
2 limes diced (into 8 pieces)
1/4 cup of fresh mint leaves
3 cups of crushed ice cubes

Method:
Pour all juices and mix well

Add red wine and sherry into a Sangria pitcher

Bruise mint leaves and add

Pour in all pieces of fruit and stir

Finally add crushed ice

Mix well and ladle into glasses

Traditionally in my home, Cook-up Rice was a Saturday meal in Guyana. It was generally served with a peppery cucumber salad, and fried fish. Sometimes a beef stew, or some fried chicken worked as a fantastic side. I really enjoy this as is with no side, except for the cucumber salad. Of course you need some Swank (home made lemonade) to wash this down.

Chan's Diwali Kheer (Sweet Rice)

1 cup of long grain rice (soaked overnight in 4 cups of water)
2 tbsp ghee (clarified butter)
5 tins of low-fat carnation milk
3 tins of condensed milk
1 cup of white raisins
1 tsp almond extract
½ cup of white sugar
3 cinnamon sticks (broken into large pieces)
12 whole cloves
½ tsp ground cardamom
1/8 tsp ground cinnamon
1/8 tsp ground nutmeg
1 & ½ cups of low-fat milk

Method:

Add ghee in a deep stock pot on medium heat

Drain soaked rice and add to pot

Saute, until water is absorbed and rice is coated with ghee

Add cinnamon sticks, cloves, ground cinnamon and nutmeg and continue to turn

Turn constantly to avoid the rice from browning

Soak raisins in hot water to plump and let this sit for 20 minutes

After 5 7 minutes of cooking, add regular low fat milk and stir

Add the carnation and condensed milk

Continue to stir, and add sugar

Cook for 2 hours on a simmer or until rice is melted an shows a thick consistency

Add raisins and continue to cook for another 20 minutes

Transfer to a serving bowl and cover until ready to serve

Tamarind Chutney

1 cup of seedless tamarind
1 cup of grated jaggery or brown sugar
1 tsp red chilli powder
1 piece cinnamon stick
1 ½ teaspoons salt
1 tsp grounded parched geera (same as cumin)
1 tsp freshly grated ginger
1/4 cup of raisins

Method:

In a saucepan bring tamarind with two cups of water to a rapid boil.

Reduce to a low simmer and cook for 7 minutes.

Leave to cool, then strain using a sieve.

Add to the tamarind pulp, raisins, cinnamon, and jaggery.

Cook on a low simmer for 25 minutes

Add salt, geera, ginger, and chili powder.

Continue cooking for another 15 minutes.

Pour into jars that have been boiled and are still hot,

seal with cover, add to a pot to stand in boiling water

on low simmering for 15 - 20 minutes.

Remove carefully with tongs, using a kitchen towel,

Store in a cool dry place

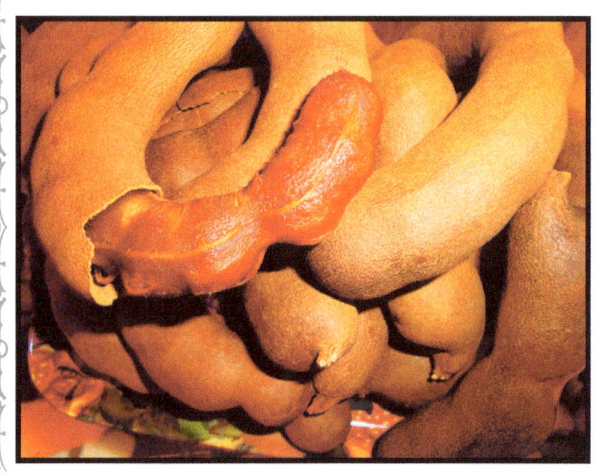

Tamarind

My dining room table is always laden with fresh fare and is usually set to reflect my mood. This is a typical presentation of Vegetable Cook-up Rice, a regular in my household, and a favorite with my sons Matthew and Martin. The red wine is always mine...

Callaloo Cook-Up

1 lb or bunch of spinach or callaloo
1 cup of pumpkin peeled, seeded, and cut into 2 inch pieces
10-12 okras, ends cut off and snipped half
1 cup of coconut milk
1 cup of rice
1 1/4 cup of water
1 ½ tspns of salt
1 tbsp of dried thyme crumbled, or fresh thyme chopped
1 medium yellow onion minced finely
1-2 wiri peppers chopped (optional)
½ tsp freshly ground black pepper
2 tbsp of vegetable or olive oil
2 blades of finely chopped scallion/ eschalot

Method:

In a large pot, saute onion for 2 minutes on medium heat

Add all ingredients, except spinach/callaloo, and scallion

Bring to a rapid boil and reduce heat low to simmer and cover

Cook for 15 minutes, then remove cover from sauce pot and

Add spinach/callaloo

Do not stir, cover and cook for an additional five minutes

Remove lid and stir

Transfer to a serving platter and top with scallions

Serve hot

Vegetable Cook-up Rice

guyana's tasty exotic   69

Yeung Chow Fried Rice

4 cups of refrigerated cooked long grain rice
2 Lap Chung sliced thinly (optional)
½ lb uncooked shrimp
1 strip of Char Sui sliced (optional)
½ Cantonese Barbeque Chicken chopped into pieces
1 tsp five spiced powder
4 tbsp light soy
1 large onion chopped
2 tbsp vegetable oil
½ tbsp of fresh ginger minced
½ tsp ground white pepper
1 cup of Chinese long bean (bora)
3 tbsp finely chopped scallions (green part only)

For shrimp:
1 tbsp Chinese rice wine
1 tsp corn starch
1/4 tsp white pepper
1 tbsp light soy
1 clove garlic minced
Combine all ingredients with shrimp
Marinate for 30 minutes

Method:
Using a wok on high heat, saute Shrimp for 2 minutes and set aside

Add Lap Chung to wok and stir fry for 1 minute, then set aside

Heat 1 tbsp oil and add onion, cook for 2 minutes and remove

Add 1 tbsp oil and long bean(bora) and stir fry for 3 minutes

Add ginger, five spiced powder, soy, rice, white pepper and stir fry

Return shrimp and Lap Chung to wok, add pork, and stir fry for 1 minute

transfer to a serving platter, place Roast chicken on top and sprinkle with scallions

Cantonese Style Orange Chicken

1 - 4 lb chicken cut into 8 pieces
½ cup orange marmalade
4 tbsp hoisin sauce
1 tbsp five spice powder
½ tsp white pepper
1 orange half thinly sliced
2 tbsp orange juice
1 tbsp orange zest
1 tbsp brown sugar
1 tbsp chopped scallions for additional flavor

Method:
Preheat oven to 375 degrees

Combine orange marmalade, hoisin sauce, five spice powder, white pepper, orange juice, oranges zest, and brown sugar

Mix well to combine

Place chicken in an oblong Pyrex dish and pour marinade,

spread generously on both sides

Place in oven and cook for 75 minutes or until all liquid is absorbed and meat is fork tender Transfer to a platter

Garnish with orange slices and with scallions

Caribe Shrimp Roll

1 pack hot dog rolls
1 lb cooked shrimp roughly chopped
½ cup Hellman's Light mayonnaise
½ cup chopped cilantro
½ tsp lime juice
½ tsp lime zest
1 tsp light soy sauce
1 tsp Dijon or yellow mustard
½ tsp cayenne pepper
1 avocado diced
½ cup of sweet mango diced
Boston or Bibb Lettuce

Method:
In a food processor add mayonnaise, cilantro, mustard,

lime juice and zest, cayenne pepper, light soy sauce

Transfer into a mixing bowl

Add shrimp, mango and avocado

Careful incorporate, and refrigerate for 1 hour

Distribute mixture generously between rolls

Top with Boston or Bibb lettuce

Serve immediately

Cucumber Tea Sandwiches

1 loaf of white bread
1 large seedless cucumber
6 oz of whipped cream cheese
1 small bunch of chives chopped
½ tsp white pepper

Method:

In a bowl combine cream cheese, white pepper, chives, and mix well

Baste mixture generously with a spatula on 2 slices of bread

Place slices of cucumber on one side and cover with to seal

Press firmly and cut away crusts to form a neat seal

Cut into 4 triangles

Spicy & Sweet Guava BBQ Sauce

1 lb of guava paste
1/4 ketchup
½ orange juice
½ cup brown sugar
1 tsp salt
1 small onion diced
3 garlic cloves diced
1 tbsp mustard
2 limes juiced
½ balsamic vinegar

Method:

Combine all ingredients

Cook and stir well until nice and thick for about 25 minutes on low to medium heat.

Curried Fish

2 lbs of Grouper or Catfish (or a fish of your choice)
1 ½ tablespoon salt
2-3 Wiri Wiri peppers or ½ Scotch Bonnet pepper
1/4 cup of chopped cilantro (optional)
1 medium onion
1 medium sized tomato
8-10 okras
1 cup of water
1 tbsp of finely chopped cilantro for garnishing

2 limes
2 tablespoons of Fish Masala (recipe in index)
2 blades of scallions
1/4 cup of celery leaves
4 cloves of garlic
1 medium sized green mango
2 tbsp vegetable oil
1 tbsp water (for curry paste)
½ of a lime (for additional garnishing)

Method:
Rinse fish with cool water and drain well

Cut into 3 inch square pieces, and place in a dish

Roll limes to soften, juice and set aside

Sprinkle 1 tbsp of salt on to fish

Pour ½ of the reserved lime juice on to fish pieces

Let this marinate for 20 minutes

Rinse fish, drain well and set aside

Peel mango, cut into wedges, and set aside

Rinse and dry okras, trim ends and set aside

In a food processor or mortar and pestle, grind the following:

Tomato, scallion, cilantro, celery leaves, peppers, onion, and garlic

Transfer into a little mixing bowl and add water and reserved lime juice

Mix well, add Fish Masala, and curry powder and form a soft paste

Heat oil in a cast iron pot or a comparable type pot

Add curry paste, and saute for about 2 - 3 minutes on medium heat

Stir to prevent sticking, add mango and okras and cook for another minute

Add fish pieces, distributing curry paste onto pieces carefully

Cook for another minute, then add water

Scrape bits from the bottom of skillet, increase heat to a rapid boil

Reduce heat to medium, add salt, stir, and cover to simmer

Cook for about 15 minutes or until a thick gravy is formed

Sprinkle with chopped cilantro and a generous squeeze of lime

Fish Quiche

2 lbs of fresh fish (Trout or White Fish)
3 eggs beaten
1/4 cup of milk
½ cup of breadcrumbs
½ tsp of white pepper
3 tbsp of melted butter
1 tsp salt
1 tbsp of fresh thyme minced
1 tbsp of fresh chopped parsley
1 tbsp of finely chopped celery leaves
1/4 cup of dried toasted breadcrumbs
½ cup grated cheddar cheese
1 large tomatoes sliced thinly, then cut into halves
1 tsp of yellow mustard
1 9"round prepared pastry dough (see index for dough recipe)

Method:
Place fish in a sauce pot with just enough water to cover

Steam for about 6 minutes

Drain and cool

Remove bones and skin

Use fingers to make flaky and into bits, and set aside

In a bowl add eggs, milk, half of the cheese, thyme, parsley, celery,

mustard, butter, salt, pepper, and fish

Use a spatula to incorporate carefully,

in order not to break fish pieces into a finer state

Place dough in a grease 9" pie dish

Pour mixture and spread evenly with a spatula

Place tomato slices overlapping each other

Drizzle the dried bread crumbs

Top with the remainder of cheddar cheese

Bake for 40 minutes at a 375-degree oven

Remove and garnish with sprigs of thyme

Cool, and serve with a small green salad and a glass of German Reisling

Whether you are in Jamaica, Bermuda, or Guyana, Peas and Rice is a big favorite. For not only is this one pot meal easy to make, it is quite filling with many variations to suit one's preference. I remember a food vendor by the name of "Small Boy", who had this little hole in the wall place in Albouystown, and he made a killer Peas and Rice, referred to by Guyanese as Cook-Up Rice. His food was finger licking good and folks joined lines to purchase it, including myself. This recipe is an ode to Small Boy, wherever he may be...

Peas and Rice Caribe Style

1 1/4 Cup of Long Grain Rice
1 Cup of Pigeon Peas (fresh or canned)
1 Cup of Stock or water
1 Cup of Coconut Milk (fresh or canned)
2 tbsp of finely chopped Thyme
1 yellow onion minced finely
1 Scotch Bonnet Pepper minced finely
1/8 tspn of ground Cinnamon
1/4 tspn of ground Black Pepper
2 small OR 1 large bouillon
½ tspn Salt
2 tbsp vegetable Oil

Method:
Heat Oil and saute Onion.

Add Peas and cook until slightly brown

Add Scotch Bonnet Pepper and saute for ½ minute

Stir well and add Rice, Cinnamon, Allspice, Black Pepper

Add Thyme, Salt, Chicken Stock, Coconut Milk, and Bouillon

Incorporate well by stirring and bring to a rapid boil

Reduce to a low fire and simmer for 20 minutes

Fluff with a fork and transfer to a serving platter

Serve with Curry Goat (optional)

Caribbean Kitchen Reference

In some Caribbean kitchens, measurements are generally done in the palm of the hand, as well as using a regular coffee or tea cup in lieu of measuring cups and spoons. Though this was not a common practice in all kitchens, it was the rustic way in which many foods were prepared in many households with great end results.

So upon testing these recipes, I threw a dash of this, a pinch of that, and pounds and pints into measuring spoons and cups for precision and conversion, of which I have added to the list below.

Dry measurements and equivalents:

1 pinch	1/8 teaspoon
2 pinches	1/4 teaspoon
4 pinches	½ teaspoon
1 dash	1 teaspoon
1 handful	1 tablespoon
½ tablespoon	1 ½ teaspoon
1/4 ounce	1 tablespoon
3 teaspoons	½ ounce
1/8 cup	2 tablespoons
1 ounce	1/4 cup
4 tablespoons	2 ounces
½ cup	8 tablespoons
4 ounces	3/4 cup
12 tablespoons	6 ounces
1 cup	½ pound
8 ounces	2 cups
1 pound	16 ounces

Liquid measurements and equivalents:

A few drops	½ teaspoon
A dash	1 tablespoon
½ tablespoon	½ teaspoon
1/4 ounce	1 tablespoon
3 teaspoons	½ ounce
1/8 cup	2 tablespoons
1 fluid ounce	1/4 cup
tablespoons	2 fluid ounces
½ cup	8 tablespoons
4 fluid ounces	3/4 cup
12 tablespoons	6 fluid ounces
1 cup	½ pound
8 fluid ounces	2 cups
1 pint	16 fluid ounces
4 cups	1 quart
2 pints	2 quarts
½ gallon	4 pints
4 quarts	1 gallon
8 pints	

Cooking Chart for Meats

Beef
Medium rare - 145 F
Medium - 160 F
Well done - 170 F

Chicken
Well done - 165 F

Duck
Well done - 170 F

Lamb
Medium rare - 145 F
Medium - 160 F
Well done - 170 F

Turkey
Done - 165

Pork
Roasts & Chops - 160F

Glossary of some of the foods of Six peoples

Amerindian

Casava Bread - Casava also known as Yucca is grated and squeezed using a large flexible sieve, know as a matapee. The juice is reserved to make cassareep. The cassava particles are then spread onto a hot metal pan, molded into a flat bread which is cooked over a fire, flipped to the other side, upon which cooking is continued until crisp, but never browned

Cassareep - Casava also known as Yucca is grated and squeezed. The liquid is reserved, and cooked until reduced to a thick, fermented sauce. The sauce becomes a dark thick substance with a distinct flavor with perservative properties, which is then used in a dish known as Pepperpot

Pepperpot - An Amerindian stew that consists of several types of wild meat, cooked slowly with herbs and cassaereep, simmered daily, never refrigerated, and served with cassava bread

Portuguese

Garlic Pork - Pieces of beef, pork, or lamb, seasoned with thymes, hot pepper, and garlic, then placed in sterilized glass jars in a vinegar brine to marinate for 3-5 days before frying until crispy

Salt Fish Cakes - Dried Cod Fish that has been regenerated with hot water, stripped into pieces, seasoned with fresh herbs and spices, along with breadcrumbs and eggs, and made into cakes and fried until golden brown

Chinese

Chow mein - Chinese noodles boiled, strained and seasoned with Chinese soy sauce, five spice powder, other seasoning, vegetables and meat to create a tasty stir fry noodle delight

Cantonese Roast

Meats - An array of meats, such as chicken, pork, and duck that has been hung to air dry, after being marinated with Chinese five spice powder, pepper, after which it is then roasted a very hot oven

African

Metemgee - An array of tropical root vegetables, okra, calalloo, meats and fish that has been simmered in coconut milk with fresh herbs and seasonings to create a hearty one pot meal

Cook Up Rice - Rice, peas, meat, fresh herbs, cooked in coconut milk creating a one pot meal with great flavor

Souse - Souse is made with calf's feet, face, and ears. It is seasoned with Scallions, lime, cucumbers, and hot peppers. This is a Saturday afternoon specialty served with Black Pudding

Indian

Roti and Curry - Roti is an Indian flat bread that is cooked on a special flat pan known as a Tawa. Curry can be made with meat, fish and or vegetables

Dhal - Yellow split peas cooked with water and Indian spices until well done and thickened, to peas soup consistency

Poulourie - An appetizer, this is also made with yellow split peas that have been soaked overnight, grounded, mixed with flour and Indian spices, then dropped by spoonfuls into hot oil, deep fried, then served with a mango or tamarind sour condiment

British

Shepherds Pie - A hearty meal consisting of meat, potatoes and vegetables, which is baked until brown and bubbly

Black Pudding - A sausage filled with rice, cows blood, hot peppers, and herb. This sausage is then boiled carefully until blood is cooked

Scones & Tea Sandwiches - Scones are like buttery biscuits and can be sweet or savory, tea sandwiches can be made with watercress, white bread and butter, or cheese, ham and cheese, and egg salad, just to list a few types, that one might find on a serving tray for 4 O'clock tea